© **Copyright 2006; a/e ProNet & J. Kent Holland, Jr.**

All rights reserved. No part of this book shall be reproduced, stored in a retrieval system or database, or transmitted by any means, electronic, mechanical, photocopying, recording, or otherwise, without written permission from the author. Contract clauses herein that are copyrighted by the AIA or EJCDC may not be further reproduced without their permission.

Cover art © Copyright 2005 by Hunt Construction Group
(CINergy Center Project - Cincinnati, OH)

Printed in the United States of America

First Printing   October 2005

Published and Distributed in the United States by:
Ardent Publications
8596 Coral Gables Lane
Vienna, VA 22182

Library of Congress Control Number: 2005903673

ISBN 0972315829

Risk Management & Contract Guide for Design Professionals

J. Kent Holland, Esq.

Ardent Publications
Vienna, Virginia

DISCLAIMER

No liability is assumed with respect to the use of the information contained herein, nor shall the publisher, distributor, author, or any employer or entity with which the author is affiliated be liable for damages or loss resulting from its use, including but not limited to actual, consequential, or incidental damages, whether foreseeable or unforeseeable. Although every precaution has been taken in the preparation of this book, the author assumes no responsibility for errors or omissions.

The opinions expressed herein are solely those of the author, and do not represent the views of a/e ProNet, any a/e ProNet member, any individual, partnership, corporation, institution of learning, or any other entity by which the author is or has been employed or affiliated.

The hypothetical situations and contract clauses discussed herein are general in nature, and the suggested responses are not meant to be the only solutions to the issues raised. Moreover, the content and comments in the text are provided for educational purposes and for general distribution, and cannot apply to any single set of specific circumstances, and should not be applied without the review and approval or your attorney.

While this book contains explanations of various legal concepts, it is not legal advice, and should not be construed or relied upon as such. It is important to remember that statutory and common law varies from state to state, and how one court may interpret the language of a contract may be different from how it will be interpreted and applied by another court in another jurisdiction.

Legal advice concerning any matter presented or discussed in this Guide should be sought from competent counsel, knowledgeable in the law of the jurisdiction in which services will be performed and under which the contract will be enforced.

Table of Contents

Acknowledgments i

About the Author ii

About *a/e ProNet* iii

Introduction v

Chapter 1 - Some Risk Management Essentials 1
1.1   Risk Avoidance
1.2   Risk Allocation
1.3   Risk Reduction

Chapter 2 - Documenting Parties' Communication 5
2.1   Written Documentation
2.2   Clear, Concise, and Temperate Language
2.3   Pre-Proposal or Pre-Bid Data and Information
        Provided by Client
2.4   Reports and Written Recommendations
2.4.1   State Foundation and Assumptions Underlying
        Opinions
2.4.2   Impact of Time Limitations
2.4.3   Identify Limitations on Information

Chapter 3 - Keeping the Records Straight 19
3.1   Benefits of Knowing How to Find Your Records
3.2   Records to Maintain
3.3   Organizing Electronic Files
3.4   Keep Attorney-Client Privileged Files Separate from
        Others
3.5   Document Contract Negotiations
3.6   Web-Based Systems
3.7   E-mail

Chapter 4 - Records Retention, Destruction, & Litigation   31
4.1   How Long Must Records be Kept?

4.2 What Documents Must be Given in Response to Discovery Requests?
4.3 Records Retention and Negligent Spoliation of Evidence
4.4 E-Mail Confidentiality and Discovery During Litigation

Chapter 5 - Purpose of Design & Construction Contracts 39

Chapter 6 - Contract Essentials 45
6.1 The Wisdom of Getting it in Writing
6.2 Basic Elements of the Professional Services Agreement
6.2.1 Scope of Services
6.2.2 Performance Schedule
6.2.3 Fee Schedule
6.2.4 General Terms and Conditions
6.3 Available Contracts Forms
6.3.1 Standard Form Agreements
6.3.2 AIA Documents
6.3.3 EJCDC Documents
6.3.4 DBIA Documents
6.3.5 Forms Created by Individual Design Professional Firms

Chapter 7 - Some Do's & Don'ts of Contract Language . 63
7.1 Use Clear Language
7.2 Words to Avoid

Chapter 8 - Marketing and Promotional Materials 65

Chapter 9 - Insurance 67
9.1 What is Covered by a Professional Liability Policy?
9.2 Indemnification Provisions Affecting Coverage
9.3 Who is Covered?

Chapter 10 - Allocating Risks Through Contract Terms & Conditions 73

Contract Clause Examples 75

Americans With Disabilities Act (ADA) 77
CAD and Electronic Media 81
Certifications 87
Changes in Design Professional's Services 91
Change Orders for Construction Work 97
Changed Conditions (Differing Site Conditions) 103
Choice of Law & Venue 107
Compliance with Law 111
Confidentiality 117
Cost Estimates 121
Damages 127
Dispute Resolution 131
Environmental Conditions 143
Incorporation by Reference 149
Indemnification 153
Inspection 163
Insurance 169
Limitation of Liability 173
Notice Requirements 177
Owner Provided Data 181
Ownership and Copyrights of Documents 187
Permits 195
Reliance on Information Provided by Others 199
Responsibility for the Services of Others 203
Schedule (Timeliness of Performance) 205
Scope of Service 211
Severability & Survival 213
Shop Drawings 217
Site Safety 221
Standard of Care 233
Termination 241
Time Limitations on Litigation 247
Waiver of Subrogation 251
Warranties and Guarantees 253

Chapter 11 - Continuing Education Courses 259

Index 281

Acknowledgments

Acknowledgment is gratefully given to a/e ProNet, its Board of Directors, and the many members who participated in creating this Guide, with special thanks to Meade Collinsworth, Warren Redeker, and Lou Moreno for sharing their professional knowledge and experience, and providing valuable insights, comments, and suggestions concerning content.

Special thanks also to Ava J. Abramowitz for her discussion in Chapter 5 on "The Purpose of Design and Construction Contracts," and to Michael C. Loulakis for his discussion in Chapter 6 concerning the Design-Build Institute of America (DBIA) contract documents.

Particular appreciation is also in order for Suzanne Harness, Managing Director and Counsel, American Institute of Architects (AIA) Contract Documents, for thoroughly reviewing the manuscript, meeting with the author, and contributing a discussion in Chapter 6 concerning the AIA contract documents.

We thank Robert J. Smith, Legal Counsel to the Engineers Joint Contract Documents Committee (EJCDC), for his participation in reviewing the manuscript. We are grateful to the AIA and the EJCDC for granting us permission to reproduce excerpts from their contract documents.

And finally, this book would not have been possible without the shepherding hand of Dan Middleton, Executive Director of a/e ProNet, and without our diligent and patient copy editor and designer, Beth Hughes.

About the Author

Kent Holland is a risk management consultant for the environmental and design professional liability unit of Arch Insurance Group, and he is Of Counsel with the law firm of Wickwire Gavin, P.C., with a practice emphasizing construction law. He provides contract reviews and risk management workshops for design professionals and has been involved in the drafting process for numerous insurance policy forms.

Mr. Holland is a frequent speaker and writer on the subject of risk management for design professionals, including several books he has authored and co-authored. He develops and maintains a construction risk management website at www.ConstructionRisk.com and publishes an electronic newsletter by the same name, analyzing recent legal cases and risk management issues.

Mr. Holland received his Juris Doctorate degree from the Villanova University School of Law in 1979. He may be reached at Kent@KentHolland.com.

About *a/e ProNet*

a/e ProNet was formed to bring together insurance professionals whose activities in their own market area had already established them as experienced, knowledgeable, and personally committed to service the design professional community. Exceptional expertise, value-added services, and independence of ties with any particular insurance company have been membership watchwords from the outset.

Since its first formal meeting in January 1988, *a/e ProNet's* membership has grown from a handful of members to a group of more than 30 firms operating on an international basis with members located in major metropolitan areas throughout the United States, and more recently in the United Kingdom. Geographical location is not a bar to membership. The absence of specialized expertise precludes consideration for membership.

Currently, some estimated 16,000 plus design firms are served by the members of *a/e ProNet,* representing a projected professional liability annual premium volume exceeding $200 million. This is a significant share of the total annual premium volume written by U.S. insurers for this specialized coverage.

These numbers are expected to grow annually irrespective of the growth of *a/e ProNet* membership. This is due to the exceptional expertise and resources available to *ProNet* members and made available to *ProNet* clients and prospective clients. Evidence of the Association's exceptional services is available on the *a/e ProNet* Website at www.aepronet.org. The *a/e ProNet* Website is one of the most comprehensive collections of a/e specialized Risk Management information and resources of its kind on the internet. Readers of this **Contract Guide** are encouraged to visit the *a/e ProNet* Website for a firsthand introduction to the extensive collection of **Practice Notes** publications, Guest Essays, and Topic of the Day professionally written articles. This **Contract Guide** is the latest example of the serious efforts of *a/e ProNet* members to bring to the design professional community the most current, cutting edge risk management resources to introduce design professionals to the legal and liability risks they may encounter in their practice. Proper utilization of this Guide will provide the reader with effective ways to eliminate, modify, and assume the identified risks with confidence they are within their insurance coverage and if not, with the prior knowledge of the risks assumed.

An added bonus to this **Contract Guide** is the AIA and Licensing Board registered Continuing Education Courses available in the back of the Guide. Readers are encouraged to take advantage of these courses if they are in need of Continuing Education credits.

As this **Contract Guide** has been written by a nationally known and respected author of other a/e Risk Management manuals, we are confident this Guide will be a valuable tool for the design firms that utilize it. Your evaluation of this **Contract Guide** as an effective and informative tool for your organization's management of legal and liability risk is of great interest to *a/e ProNet*. Your comments are welcome. Please feel free to contact us at *a/e ProNet*, 3543 Somerset Circle, Kissimmee, FL 34746. We are pleased that you are participating in the learning experience provided by this Guide and wish you good luck in the completion of the Continuing Education Courses should you elect to participate.

The Officers, Directors, and Members of *a/e ProNet*

Introduction

This contract guide will assist design professionals in better understanding key issues concerning risks and liabilities potentially arising out of contracts, communication, and documentation.

Space did not permit inclusion of every contract term and condition that may impact risk. Approximately 34 clauses that may be of particular concern are discussed. For each of these clauses, one or more key issues is considered. Please note that this is not intended to be a comprehensive review. The conclusions are not intended to provide legal or other professional advice. Obtain the advice of counsel before drafting clauses for specific projects.

Most of the example clauses are excerpts from longer clauses that are copyrighted by the American Institute of Architects (AIA) or the Engineers Joint Contract Documents Committee (EJCDC) and are not to be reproduced or used without authorization of the appropriate organization.

In addition to discussing example contract clauses, we have included a discussion of risk management of communication and documentation. As you will see from the litigation examples referenced, many claims against design professionals could be avoided or mitigated through better communication and documentation. This is such an important issue that entire seminars are devoted to it.

At the conclusion of the *Guide*, there are three continuing education exams. To receive credit for completing the exams, contact a/e ProNet at http://www.aeProNet.org, and sign up for the continuing education course.

Chapter 1

Some Risk Management Essentials
1.1   Risk Avoidance
1.2   Risk Allocation
1.3   Risk Reduction

Risk managers often speak of three primary means of risk management: risk avoidance, risk allocation, and risk reduction. Key points concerning these three methods are briefly presented below.

1.1   Risk Avoidance

The most obvious way to avoid risk is to not perform services. Don't accept a bad contract. In reality, however, design professionals who want to be retained for assignments are often only too anxious to sign contracts—even if they contain onerous terms and conditions. Because accepting contracts and performing services are critical to a design professional's livelihood, the key is to recognize and avoid those risks that are unacceptable.

Terms and conditions that contain onerous risks—especially risks that are uninsurable under a professional liability policy—should be identified before the contract is signed and revised so as to be acceptable and insurable to the greatest extent possible. If it isn't possible to negotiate a reasonable contract, the safe course of action may very well be to decline the contract and the project.

To accept uninsurable risks is to bet the firm on the assumption that the risks will not materialize or that the ones that do will be minimal. The client who insists on shifting owner and contractor risks to the design firm is often the client who is most likely to have unreasonable expectations. That same client may also be quickest to take you to court when things don't go as hoped. In such circumstances, the best decision you can make in managing your firm might be to reject a bad contract.

Risk avoidance also includes rejecting requests for your services on projects that fall outside your area of knowledge and experience. Even if your firm has the requisite experience, the personnel with that expertise may be tied up on other projects. In both situations, it is usually safer to reject the project than to attempt to have inexperienced personnel perform the services.

In the busy construction market of the past several years, it has not been uncommon to see design firms submit proposals on multiple projects—expecting to be awarded no more than one contract—and being awarded contracts on multiple projects. This might seem great until you realize that your key personnel are unavailable because they are still working on another project, for a different owner, in a distant location. This has been particularly problematic when construction contractors are late in completing their work, delaying the completion of the design services during construction, and thereby preventing the release of your key personnel to move over to other projects.

1.2 Risk Allocation

In allocating risks by contract terms and conditions, the goal is to allocate the specific risks to the party with the best ability to manage them. Although a contract can assign ownership of risks to any party, there can be serious adverse consequences if a party assumes risks it can't manage. A design firm, for example, isn't in a position to manage site safety responsibilities that most appropriately belong to the construction contractor. Despite the practicalities, however, of who is actually in the best position to manage site safety, if the design firm agrees to such responsibility by contract, the designer may be found liable for site safety by courts and possibly the Department of Labor.

To be reasonable, a contract must be reasonable for all parties involved. If a contract attempts to shift all the risks to one party or the other, it will create problems on the project. A one-sided contract is likely to cause hard feelings during contract administration. It may also increase the likelihood of claims turning into litigation. As a practical matter, this means parties are better served by negotiators who don't try to negotiate a contract that unreasonably shifts risk to someone who can't logically manage it or accept legal responsibility for it. Such risk transfer will cause problems in the long run, and may even create uninsurable losses and claims.

In evaluating who the various risks should be assigned to, parties can develop a table or list of responsibilities and risks to more easily see which risks most logically belong to each party. For example, site safety typically falls to the construction contractor. Easements and rights-of-way, as well as site data, including geotechnical information, may logically be allocated to the project owner. Responsibility for exercising due care in the planning and designing of a project generally falls to the design professional performing those services.

Problems begin when any of these risks are allocated to the party that is not technically responsible for the related services. Unless you are in a position to manage a particular risk, it is not appropriate for you to accept contractual liability for that risk.

1.3 Risk Reduction

After you have decided to accept risks by taking on the project, and you have negotiated as best you can for a reasonable allocation of risks, you are ready for the next step of risk management: risk reduction. Risk reduction involves taking preventative actions to decrease the probability, frequency, and severity of losses. Sometimes called "proactive," these activities can be planned in advance to respond to risks that are known and that are manageable when encountered. What these proactive steps will include depends upon the nature of the project, the location, and the risk.

Chapter 2

Documenting Communication between the Parties

2.1　Written Documentation
2.2　Clear, Concise, and Temperate Language
2.3　Pre-Proposal or Pre-Bid Data and Information Provided by Client
2.4　Reports and Written Recommendations
2.4.1　State Foundation and Assumptions Underlying Opinions
2.4.2　Impact of Time Limitations
2.4.3　Identify Limitations on Information

2.1　Written Documentation

When it comes to determining what was said, when it was said, and who decided what, the best evidence generally is written documentation. This includes correspondence, memoranda, notes, faxes, and e-mails. As discussed elsewhere in this book, written documentation can be particularly important to prove you complied with contract requirements. Written evidence that you met all contractual notice requirements and obtained proper and timely approvals can be vital to your success in presenting claims or defending against them. It can also prove you gave sufficient information to others so they could make intelligent decisions and possibly even assume the risk of their decisions.

Many initial communications between the parties will take place orally in the ordinary course of conversation on the project. Unless these oral conversations are somehow reduced to writing in the form of meeting minutes, memoranda, or correspondence, their content and value may be lost.

If you are orally communicating information that you believe is important to project decisions, document it in writing and preserve it. Likewise, if you are receiving oral communication that has significance to the project, make a written record of that conversation. You may, otherwise, find yourself in a dispute several years after the project has been completed, when memories have faded, and you will have nothing to prove how the decisions were made.

A discussion of case examples later in this text explains how a project owner in one HVAC case denied receiving a memorandum from the design professional warning of the risk of substituting equipment. This type of a denial could be avoided if a record of the memorandum proved that the communication had been made.

As suggested earlier, a record can be a fax confirmation notice, an e-mail confirmation notice, a certified mail-return receipt, or a note from the client acknowledging the design professional's recommendation. Even if no written record is made to confirm that the recommendation was received by the client, there may be other methods to prove that the client received the notice and acted upon it.

A follow-up note to the client referencing the written recommendation can be useful. This can state something to the effect that you are sending it to confirm that you sent the earlier memo and will be taking action in accordance with any understandings that may have been reached concerning those recommendations. You could also raise the issue at a formal project meeting and have the matter, including the fact that the written recommendation was made, recorded into the meeting minutes.

Even telephone logs and notes are useful as contemporaneous business records to show that a conversation occurred concerning the recommendation contained in the memorandum that was never formally acknowledged by the client. By doing these things, you are making it more difficult for the client to later deny having received the written recommendation.

Documents that should be maintained in well-organized files for ready access include:

- Requests for Information (RFIs);
- Telephone logs;
- Change order requests and change orders;
- Inspection Logs (i.e., monitoring or reviewing reports);
- Daily reports (e.g., weather, laborers, etc.);
- Safety reports;
- Payment requests;
- Certifications; and
- Lien waivers.

These are some of the more significant types of documents, but this is by no means an exclusive or exhaustive list. Other documentation that has proved invaluable in prosecuting claims or defending against them include tape recordings of pre-bid conferences, photographs of job progress, and video tapes of job progress.

2.2 Clear, Concise, and Temperate Language

It goes without saying that we should not put anything in writing for distribution outside our own firm that we believe could in any way embarrass or damage us. This same principle should be applied to all notes, memos, yellow sticky notes, and e-mail notes that are intended for viewing only by those inside the firm.

If attorneys pursue document discovery in a claim that involves your firm, you may be sure that any damaging comment, observation, or statement contained in your internal files and memoranda will be among the first items sought by the reviewing attorneys.

The risk management principles applicable to formal documentation between parties also apply to the language we use internally in reports, correspondence, memoranda, telephone logs, meeting minutes, yellow sticky notes, and any other written materials intended for in-house use.

2.3 Pre-Proposal or Pre-Bid Data and Information Provided By Client

Design professionals should be able to rely upon geotechnical reports, site data, client program requirements, and other information provided by the client. Standard form contracts for both construction and design professional services generally state the terms under which a firm may rely upon that information. Not all contracts, however, permit such reliance. Recent contracts generated by project owners have included language stating that any site conditions information provided by the owner is done so merely for general information and shall not be deemed a part of the contract, nor may it be relied upon by designers or contractors. Some of these contracts state that the designer or bidder is expected to perform its own site investigation and make its own determinations of what will be encountered at the site.

By disclaiming any responsibility for the information it provides, the owner may be able to avoid paying for additional services or change orders. Several courts, including those in Florida and Texas, have recently published decisions holding that municipal governments had no duty to grant change orders based on differing site conditions where the contracts had expressly disclaimed reliance upon site information provided by the owner.

Despite a differing site conditions clause in the construction contract, one court held that the contractor couldn't argue for a differing site condition based upon misleading and inaccurate information provided with geotechnical reports that were included with the Invitation for Bid (IFB). This was because the contract included a separate clause stating that all reports and information provided with the IFB were for general information purposes only and not to be relied upon by the bidders. That clause further stated that the reports and information were expressly excluded from the contract and that the owner was making no representations of site conditions whatsoever.

An owner's refusal to allow bidders to rely upon documentation and data provided by the owner may adversely impact the design professional. A contractor that is denied recovery under a differing site condition clause may find creative ways to argue its damages were actually caused by acts, errors, and omissions of the design professional. Or it might argue that there were misrepresentations by the design professional or interference by the design professional with the contractor's means, methods, and procedures of performance. In a number of states, contractors may seek recovery directly against the design firm for their damages.

Denying a contractor's right to rely on site information documentation may cause an increase in claims and litigation. This is because to get around the unreasonable contract provision, contractors are forced to find creative ways to make themselves whole from the loss they will otherwise suffer. Bidders that are contractually barred from relying upon information provided with the IFB may seek to include in their bids extra costs for unknown site condition contingencies. This may adversely impact the design professional who has committed to designing a facility for a specified construction cost budget.

Bids may exceed the budget if the contractor fears there is a real likelihood of incurring costs it can't recover by change order. If the design firm provides the owner with a project budget and estimates of construction costs that are exceeded by the high bids, that design professional may find itself redesigning the project (at its own costs) in order to get the contractor's price within the budget. Design firms need to take this into consideration when agreeing to responsibility for "cost estimates" and redesigning a facility to bring it within budget. This is discussed later under the topic of cost estimates.

The key points to remember are that design professionals and contractors need to understand how documentation provided by the owner in advance of accepting professional proposals and contractor bids may be relied upon, and how contract language may affect how much reliance, if any, can be placed on such information and documentation.

Assuming that you are entitled to rely upon the documentation, it is important that the records that you generate in your files at the time of preparing your proposal or bid refer to those documents and show that you relied upon them.

As a design professional, you may get an additional benefit from referring to these documents in the proposal that you submit to the owner. You will be able to demonstrate the underlying assumptions upon which you have based your proposal. If the owner subsequently requests you to perform services differing from what was anticipated based upon the documentation provided to you in advance of your proposal, you may be able to use that documentation to prove that you are being required to perform additional services entitling you to additional fees.

2.4 Reports and Written Recommendations

Put recommendations in writing, including an explanation of the potential benefits of following the recommendations and the potential risks of failing to do so. If alternative solutions or recommendations are available, conveying that information to the client, in writing, facilitates informed and well-reasoned decisions by the client. This has the added advantage of later showing a client or court that you provided your services reasonably and that the client made certain decisions assuming appropriate risks for their project program and budget.

Enough detail should be provided in the written recommendation so that the client cannot assert that it did not understand the ramifications of the decision it was making.

In one example of a claim against an architect, the owner asserted that the architect was responsible for all damages caused by the failure of the Heating, Air Conditioning, and Ventilation (HVAC) system to meet the performance requirements of the building. In its defense, the architect asserted that the owner had overruled its advice to reject the "or equal" equipment substitution that was being offered by the construction contractor.

The architect in this HVAC case proved it had provided a written recommendation to reject the equipment. The owner acknowledged it received the recommendation, but argued that it was so bland and devoid of detail that it failed to provide adequate information and details on which to reject the equipment. According to the owner, the language seemed equivocal and did not contain facts, figures, or data to persuade it to reject the equipment that was promised to save it money. The owner argued that if the architect felt so strongly that the equipment should be rejected, it should have made its recommendation so clear and obvious (with scientific reasoning to support it) that the owner would have made the right decision. The owner argued that the design firm was negligent for failing to provide a more forceful recommendation. It also argued that the firm was negligent for ultimately approving the installation of the HVAC system.

In another case involving an HVAC system, the design firm provided a detailed written memorandum to the owner recommending the rejection of equipment. Again, the owner decided to accept the equipment despite that recommendation. When the equipment failed, the owner sought to recover the cost of its damages from the architect.

The design firm in this case defended itself by asserting that it had given its client appropriate information by way of a written memorandum, and that the client had assumed the risk of failure by accepting the "or equal" equipment. A copy of the memorandum was in the architect's files, but the project owner denied receiving it. Fortunately for the design firm, a copy of a fax confirmation was eventually found in the architect's files. It showed a copy of the first page of the memo with the fax telephone number, date, number of pages transmitted, and delivery confirmation printed neatly across its top. Because of this evidence, the matter came to a prompt conclusion, with the architect avoiding any liability.

These cases demonstrate the need to put recommendations in writing, and to provide appropriately detailed information. They also serve as a warning to preserve written evidence that the design firm made appropriate recommendations and that the client received them.

It goes without saying that it isn't necessary or practical to send everything certified mail, return receipt requested. You can communicate and document that communication without antagonizing the client. It's advisable to obtain written responses from your clients regarding your recommendations. These do not have to be overly formal. In many situations, a simple note or e-mail acknowledging receipt of the recommendation will be adequate—provided that you properly file this documentation in an appropriate folder for future reference.

Keep in mind that in the example above, the design firm that eventually got out of the case by producing a fax confirmation spent a lot of money in legal fees and wasted a lot of time in the months prior to finding that piece of paper. Keeping such documents organized so they can be easily found is the key.

If the client does not respond in writing, create your own paper record showing that he received the recommendation. For example, send a short follow-up memorandum such as a "speed memo," fax, or e-mail to the client reiterating that you gave him a written recommendation, and mentioning any conversations you and the client may have had pertaining to that recommendation and any related decisions that were made by the client. If the client later denies receiving the original recommendation, these kinds of confirmation notes will be helpful in persuading both the client, and possibly the court, that the original recommendation was received.

Nothing in the above examples is intended to suggest that owners don't act ethically. It is simply a fact of life on large projects that with multiple people working in the owner's office as well as in the trailers of the design professionals and contractors, papers are sometimes misrouted or misplaced before they are read by the appropriate people. If oral communication is not followed with written confirmation, it may be difficult or impossible to reconstruct what happened if a subsequent dispute is later litigated.

Even if all the right people on the project had excellent oral communication about decisions to be made, when litigation later ensues the individuals may have long since forgotten the project details. This is where maintenance of written documentation becomes especially vital. It memorializes what went on even after memories have faded or the individuals involved are no longer accessible.

2.4.1 State Foundation and Assumptions Underlying Opinions

When drafting a report offering a professional opinion, state the foundation and assumptions upon which the opinion is based. Reference information that was provided by the client or others for your use. Reference, too, the basic assumptions that you made based upon the client's program for the project and information provided to you.

If there are limitations impacting your ability to formulate an opinion, note these limitations in the report. Budget restrictions, for example, impact the design and construction. In instances where you would propose something too expensive for the owner's restrictive budget, point this out in a written report so the client can make a well-informed decision on how to proceed.

2.4.2 Impact of Time Limitations

Time limitations may impact your ability to conduct the full research and investigation you would typically do on a similar project. There have been cases, for example, where property assessment investigations were rushed because the purchaser of real estate waited until the day before settlement to contract with a firm to perform the investigation. In one case, instead of postponing the real estate settlement, the purchasers contracted a consultant to perform a Phase I environmental site assessment of multiple parcels of industrial land only three days before the real estate closing date. The consultant agreed to perform these services, subject to certain disclaimers and conditions. Its contract terms included a statement that the site assessment report would state that the services were limited by the time restrictions and that this affected the completeness and reliability of the information presented. The client also agreed to indemnify and hold harmless the consultant from damages and claims arising out of the consultant's services.

2.4.3 Identify Limitations on Information

Limitations on the information, data, and site access provided by the client should be identified in writing in the report and recommendations. A building owner requested an architect to prepare a report estimating what it would cost to renovate part of an old building into new office space. A limitation was placed on the architect's access to the premises that would impact its ability to give an opinion: the owner forbade the architect from removing ceiling tiles to determine whether there was asbestos in the plenum.

Unless it knew what was above the ceiling tiles, the architect could not provide an estimate of construction costs with a significant degree of reasonable probability. If asbestos was later discovered in the ceiling and had to be removed as part of the renovation, the architect's original opinion of probable costs could be too low.

In this example, the architect accepted the contract with those conditions. It drafted a preliminary sketch of renovations and provided a preliminary estimate of costs. This estimate, however, included a boldly stated caveat that the architect was not making any warranties, guarantees, or representations concerning the estimate in the event that any additional work needed to be performed as a result of anything that could not be observed by the architect in the area at or above the ceiling tiles.

By clearly stating the limitations upon its access to the building and the limitation on information, the architect hoped to limit its client's (or others') ability to rely upon its report. Stating such a limitation is one risk management tool that may give the architect some protection in this situation. Other architects in a similar situation might manage the risk by declining, thereby avoiding the potential liability that could arise later. This becomes a matter of prudent client selection.

When professionals work for clients who choose to close their eyes to environmental issues impacting their property, they may come under pressure to issue reports that do not state their findings and opinions with the degree of clarity and forcefulness that they deem ethically appropriate. Some environmental regulations create an independent duty for consultants with knowledge of an on-going pollution release to notify government agencies about it. This type of situation is discussed below in the analysis of the confidentiality clause.

Conditions in the consultant's contract with its client attempting to limit such disclosures will not excuse the consultant from meeting its independent duty to the governing agencies. For this reason, if there is a clause in your contract addressing confidentiality of information and documents acquired by the consultant from the client, it should be drafted in such a manner as to allow you to provide to others the information that is legally required.

Chapter 3

Keeping the Records Straight

- 3.1 Benefits of Knowing How to Find Your Records
- 3.2 Records to Maintain
- 3.3 Organizing Electronic Files
- 3.4 Keep Attorney-Client Privileged Files Separate from Others
- 3.5 Document Contract Negotiations
- 3.6 Web-Based Systems
- 3.7 E-mail

3.1 Benefits of Knowing How to Find Your Records

Being able to promptly locate records can instantly end potential claims. As previously described in Section 2.4, a building owner sued a design firm, alleging that the design firm failed to properly advise of the risk of accepting an "or equal" equipment substitution offered by the contractor. The design firm asserted it had given the owner a detailed memorandum explaining why the equipment should be rejected, and that the owner had ignored that advice at its own peril. In response, the owner claimed that it had never received such a memorandum. After months of document discovery and depositions, someone finally located in the design firm's files a "fax confirmation" of the missing memorandum.

The fax confirmation showed a small copy of the first page of the fax, as well as the date it was sent, to whom it was sent, and the number of pages received. In light of this evidence, the matter was promptly dismissed.

If a copy of the missing document had been made available to the project owner at the outset, it's likely the suit never would have been filed. Giving the owner the benefit of presumed honesty, it seems likely that the warning memo was misplaced or misfiled so that the owner's principals were not aware of its existence when the problems with the substitute equipment began to surface and demands and claims were made against the design firm. If the design firm had filed its own copy of that memorandum in a logical place, clear and quick communication with the owner would have been possible and the misunderstanding that led to the litigation could have been avoided.

Maintain project documentation in a manner so that it can be easily retrieved. This makes good sense from a claims and litigation point of view. But more than that, it enhances communication and makes it possible to more efficiently manage the project during design and construction if the parties can quickly locate documents and use them in making their decisions.

Good document management enhances project quality control and provides a means to benchmark changes that are being made to original program requirements, drawings, and contract agreements. Time spent in establishing and maintaining a logical document control system will prevent time from being wasted later in looking for information and documents that have been misplaced, misfiled, lost, or unintentionally destroyed.

Records that are maintained contemporaneously in the ordinary course of business can serve as invaluable evidence in proving what communications took place on a project.

3.2 Records to Maintain

Documents and information need to be managed. This is not the same thing as just keeping everything forever. Nor is it sufficient to throw everything into boxes and put them into a self-storage facility to be forgotten.

Documents maintained in a logical, easily accessible manner can become vital tools in your day-to-day business not only on the project to which they pertain, but in performing services on other projects as well. If you have performed calculations and completed research on one project, the calculations and research may very well have applicability on your other projects.

Even without creating a subject matter index or filing system, you may be able to remember files that you personally worked on that can provide useful information to assist you in performing services on other projects. But others in your office who don't know about your files won't have access to this information unless it is maintained someplace other than your memory. By creating (and maintaining) a basic indexing system (manual or electronic), a firm can make records more accessible to everyone in the firm. Computer software programs can facilitate the searching of words or tables of contents in certain electronic documents. Even without sophisticated software, much can be done to organize records for future reference.

With time and age, memories fade, but the recorded, filed, written word lives on. Establish a system to access records and you reduce the amount of time and work needed to perform the new services. It also provides some enhanced quality control—particularly if the previous files had proved to be winners. This translates into more cost-effective services for the current client. When these notebooks are placed on the library shelves for others in the office to use, and when electronic files are put onto compact disks (CDs) where they can be accessed by others, the benefits are multiplied. (Note that if you give up ownership and copyright of your work product to the project owner, you may deprive yourself of the ability to re-use your own work on other projects and defeat the benefits referenced above.)

3.3 Organizing Electronic Files

For easy access and retrieval, your electronic data files—including drawings, specifications, correspondence, memoranda, e-mails, and other types of documents—should be carefully filed in electronic folders on either a computer network or hard drive as well as on specifically labeled diskettes or CDs. If you are operating in an office environment, saving the files to a network is usually the safer course because networks are typically backed up more frequently than hard drives.

If your documents are co-mingled with electronic files from other projects or other general files, you may be required to give the requesting counsel access to your entire computer or e-mail system, unintentionally giving them access to sensitive information that is not even related to the case at hand. This could even be embarrassing if you have been keeping personal information and correspondence on your computer. Keep project specific files separate and apart from all other non-related files.

If you're using your home computer to do work for your employer, understand that the electronic files that you are creating for your employer's business become the responsibility of your employer for purposes of document control and document discovery. If you don't want to risk sharing the contents of your entire computer with strangers (and attorneys opposing your firm), it is advisable that all data related to your employer's business be kept in separate electronic folders while you are working on them, and then moved onto diskettes and removed from your computer's hard drive.

3.4 Keep Attorney-Client Privileged Files Separate From Others

If you're receiving advice from legal counsel during your project, it's important that correspondence between you and your counsel be maintained in a manner which will enable you to distinguish them from your general office files later. They should be marked as "confidential", "attorney-client privileged," "attorney work product," or other such designations so that you and others in your office will recognize that these documents are not to be given to a requester during discovery before your attorney has an opportunity to review them. If these documents are copied and put into numerous files around the office or jobsite trailer, there is a significant chance that some of them will be inadvertently revealed during discovery.

It is not the purpose of this book to study the details of the attorney-client privilege, or the ethics of how to handle privileged documentation that may be inadvertently given to the requester. It is better to manage the documentation so that it does not become necessary to argue over it later. By keeping documents properly segregated, your attorney will be able to review them and make a decision concerning how they are to be handled during discovery.

Typically, your attorney will provide a letter to the requester identifying the documents for which the privilege is claimed. This permits the parties to argue over the matter before a judge, if necessary, but it at least prevents the documents from getting into the hands of the requester unless and until a judge orders them to be released.

3.5 Document Contract Negotiations

The "parol evidence" rule generally prevents evidence from outside the four corners of a signed contract from being used during litigation to attempt to change or alter the terms of the contract. Despite this rule, however, there may be times that documentation between the contract parties may be accepted by a court as evidence.

In one case, the architect and property owner exchanged multiple versions of contracts for designing and building a large house. While the architect started its design, the parties continued haggling over the contract terms. They never signed a contract. Ultimately, the owner terminated and replaced the architect. The second architect used the original architect's design documents to complete the final design and construct the house.

In a suit alleging copyright infringement, the original architect was permitted by the court to present a series of letters and draft contracts that had been transmitted back and forth between the architect and owner. These persuaded the court that the architect did not intend to give up ownership and copyright to the drawings. This case demonstrates the importance of maintaining copies of documents that were generated prior to contract finalization. These can, in some cases, assist the parties and the court in determining the intent of the parties.

3.6 Web-Based Systems

Web-based project management systems are becoming widely used on large construction projects, and even for projects that are not so large. A survey by one provider of web-based systems found that the reasons customers used their system included: (a) it plays a role in eliminating or reducing the barriers and delay points in communications, workflow, and processing information and documentation; (b) it reduces claims and litigation; and (c) it increases productivity.

With respect to increasing productivity, web-based systems have been credited with: (a) making it quicker to submit and turnaround RFIs; (b) reducing barriers in communications; (c) automating document creation; and (d) reducing the time it takes to find files and documents. 99 percent of the survey respondents stated that the system has improved document management and thus improved the firm's ability to manage risks and reduce claims and litigation.

Using electronic data and storage, it is possible to store all kinds of documents—correspondence, RFIs, minutes, notes, and logs—with relatively little effort for long periods of time. The integrity of the data is better maintained when the data is burned onto a CD, rather than saved onto a floppy disk.

Because electronic data tends to lose integrity over time, however, it may be advisable to duplicate the disks periodically over the years of storage. It is also generally advisable to maintain hard copies of the final instruments of service in order to have a standard against which to benchmark any electronic files that may have been given to the A/E's client or others. In fact, retaining the hard copies may the best (or even only) way to protect against a client's future suit that alleges the electronic data is defective.

3.7 E-mail

E-mail as a form of project documentation runs the gamut from being highly effective to extremely dangerous or even disastrous for the unwary. It is so fast and easy to use that it has become the principal mode of communication on many projects. Some firms swear by it and others swear at it. Why is there such a difference of opinion and why are the results so variable?

E-mail can be a good way to communicate. With oral communication, the speaker may not be certain that the "listener" really understood and received the message the speaker intended to send. With e-mail, you see, in writing, what someone is saying. You get to respond—in writing. And the other party can fire back a quick note telling you that you misunderstood and got the meaning all wrong. With a quick series of written messages, the parties can easily figure out (and even document) what each is saying and come to an agreement on what they intend to do.

Participants in construction projects must understand that when they communicate by e-mail, they are creating a document that may very well become a project record. Such a document may be used as key evidence in proving or defending claims. E-mail may be entered into evidence in litigation. With that in mind, it must be handled with due care. Some simple rules for dealing with e-mail include:

(a) Be careful what you write. Think before you automatically type the first thoughts that go through your mind. Don't write anything that you would not be proud to see published in the newspaper the next day.

(b) Don't be too informal. Be careful, for example, about the use of politically incorrect language, jokes, and remarks that may seem funny to you but boorish to others. O.J. Simpson was found "not guilty" by a jury that probably couldn't help but be angry about prejudicial remarks made by the key investigating detective for Los Angeles. Microsoft was found liable for anti-competitive practices by a trial court judge who later told the press that Bill Gates' e-mail messages proved he had been less than forthcoming in his oral testimony. Ironically, the judge's comments proved to be imprudent, and an appellate court accepted an appeal from Microsoft based at least in part on its concern about the judge's comments.

(c) Check your spelling and grammar—including punctuation—before you click "send." Write with the thought that this may be the only document a judge or jury will ever see in support of some issue of vital importance to the case. Provide a subject matter line, an addressee line, a proper salutation, and a proper closing.

(d) Get approval first. If your document was a memorandum rather than an e-mail and the agreement of others would be necessary before you distributed it, get those individuals to concur with your e-mail before you send it.

(e) Don't add additional services to your scope based on e-mails from people who do not have the contractual authority to assign additional services or approve change orders. E-mail messages are not deemed acceptable substitutes for properly executed approvals for additional services or properly executed change orders.

(f) If your contract calls for the use of specified procedures for requesting information and scope changes, use those procedures. Don't use e-mail as a substitute.

(g) Organize your outgoing and incoming e-mail into electronic folders for easy access and retrieval. If you co-mingle personal and work-related e-mails, you may be required to provide all of your e-mail messages during litigation.

(h) Print e-mail messages and put them into appropriate files for future reference. Electronic folders may be accidentally destroyed or lost. If the message is evidence of some decision or matter of potential significance, it should be saved with other documents addressing that issue in a form that will not be accidentally or inadvertently lost.

(i) Delete e-mail from your system and erase it from any back-up tapes or other disks, computers, and servers in a manner consistent with your corporate records purging/retention policy.

Contrary to what some people think, e-mail is not just a temporary document that lives in the nether world of the electronic universe. Even after e-mail messages have been deleted from your computer, they may still be retrieved from a server in some other location.

Another confounding issue is that the e-mail you thought was a private communication between you and one other person may get forwarded either intentionally or accidentally to others. Before you know it, your little message is being read by half the world. You might recall that during the Senate hearings of Oliver North regarding the Iran-Contra scandal, senators demanded to see his e-mail. He responded that it had all been deleted from his computer much earlier. To his surprise, the government was able to use some simple disk utility programs to resurrect his dead e-mails. It seems that e-mails have a life of their own.

To permanently destroy e-mail, consult with an experienced IT adviser. There are ways to delete it, erase it, and re-record over it to make its deletion more permanent. But be careful that you don't erase e-mails that may be subject to discovery requests in pending claims. This is discussed in greater detail in Chapter 4.

Chapter 4

Records Retention, Destruction, & Litigation

4.1 How Long Must Records be Kept?
4.2 What Documents Must be Given in Response to Discovery Requests?
4.3 Records Retention and Negligent Spoliation of Evidence
4.4 E-Mail Confidentiality and Discovery During Litigation

4.1 How Long Must Records be Kept?

Time periods established by state statutes of limitations and statutes of repose can be useful guides in determining how long to maintain project records. State statutes of repose typically bar claims that are brought more than a specified number of years after substantial completion of construction.

Time periods vary from state to state, with each state statute being different with regard to the time limit, who is covered by it, and for what kinds of services or work. As a general rule, if a statute of repose applies to your services or work, you should maintain significant project records at least through the end of the time period established under that statute. It may be prudent, however, to maintain records for an even longer period. If you are working under a contract for a federal, state, or local government or agency, for example, you may have statutory or regulatory obligations to maintain your records for a significant number of years beyond what you might normally expect.

4.2 What Documents Must be Given in Response to Discovery Requests?

When you receive a document production request in the course of a claim or litigation, you are required to provide copies or access to not only those documents that are part of your "official file," but also to those copies that may be in "working files," desk drawers, job-site trailers, workers' homes, computers at the office and home, and any other documents that pertain to the request. As owner of these records, you have the responsibility to locate them and make them available to those who are requesting them through discovery.

There have been a number of cases where the documents most vital to the plaintiff's case were found in the home of one of the defendant's employees. If the plaintiff locates such a document after the defendant denied its existence or otherwise failed to produce it, the court could impose sanctions against the defendant.

In federal courts, as well as in many state jurisdictions, parties to litigation are required to provide the other party with all documents relevant to the case even if not requested to do so by the opposing counsel. This creates an affirmative duty on each party and requires due diligence in reviewing your records and providing access to the other side. This duty makes it all the more important that you establish and follow a formal records retention policy so that you do not unnecessarily create an obligation to give someone records that should have long since been destroyed.

4.3 Records Retention and Negligent Spoliation of Evidence

There can be serious liability and potential sanctions for intentionally destroying evidence to avoid discovery of damaging information. The newspapers are full of reports about corporations and accounting firms that have allegedly destroyed records in order to prevent shareholders, courts, and even congressional committees from seeing those records which might contain embarrassing or damaging information. In some particularly egregious situations, it is argued that the destruction of records may even constitute a crime punishable with prison sentences.

Courts in some states recognize a tort of negligent spoliation of evidence. *Foster v. Lawrence Memorial Hospital*, 809 F. Supp. 831 (D.Kan.). Some of the factors considered by the courts in deciding whether to impose liability for negligently destroying evidence include the following: (1) there was a duty to maintain the evidence imposed either by law or contract; (2) a potential claim or law suit existed; (3) evidence has been destroyed; (4) the ability of the plaintiff to prove its case has been significantly impaired by the destruction of documentation; and (5) the plaintiff has suffered damages as a result of the document destruction. In *Kirkland v. NYCHA*, 236 A.D. 170, 666 NYS 2d 609, a New York court held that dismissal of a suit was an appropriate sanction against a litigant who disposed of evidence before its adversary had an opportunity to inspect it. This was held to be so regardless of whether the destruction was done intentionally or negligently.

Implementing a document retention policy and practices to consistently follow that policy are important risk management tools. Records might be routinely purged from your files and destroyed as part of your standard business practices. It might be deemed inappropriate to destroy the same records in the absence of an established procedure.

At some point, you may be in litigation where the plaintiff asserts that you destroyed records that once had been a part of your files. In such a situation, the court may consider not only whether you had a records retention/records destruction policy, but whether the specific destruction of records at issue was done pursuant to that policy, and whether the records were destroyed before or after you knew of the dispute. A records retention policy that is designed and carried out in good faith in the ordinary course of business may provide you an excellent defense to claims of spoliation of evidence. But remember that if you are in litigation or a dispute with either your client or a third party, or if there is an investigation or audit by a governmental agency, you must preserve the records rather than following the scheduled document destruction policy.

Once a records retention and purging policy has been established, it is important to consistently review your records on a periodic basis to make sure you comply with the policy. Purge and destroy those records that the policy states are to be purged, and faithfully file and maintain those records that are still to be maintained pursuant to that same policy.

Firms have gotten into trouble for destroying records on the eve of discovery by an opposing party even though they may have been able to destroy those same records years earlier pursuant to the firms' formal records retention policy. A records retention policy is no good unless you use it contemporaneously and consistently. In fact, a records retention policy can be used against you if you destroy records in a manner inconsistent with that policy. We need to apply record retention policies consistently to each project and to all of the documents covered by the policy.

When purging records from your files in the ordinary course of business, pursuant to a proper records retention policy, care should be exercised in how the records are disposed. Copies of confidential client records should not be thrown into the trash or recycle bin where they might be improperly viewed and used by other individuals. They should be shredded or otherwise destroyed. There have been unfortunate situations where careless disposal has resulted in client-confidential information being released into the hands of the public.

We see then that records can protect you in the event of misunderstandings by others on the project, and can help you to prosecute or defend a case in the event of litigation. Some forms of documentation may also hurt you, especially if they have been imprudently written or maintained. Create clear and temperate communication through written and electronic documentation. This will help you proactively manage any future disputes and litigation and improve the communication and management within your firm and with your clients and others.

4.4 E-Mail Confidentiality and Discovery During Litigation

As a general rule, computerized data is discoverable. Thus, even if a party produces a hard copy of electronic evidence, he or she may still be required to produce the electronic version. Recent examples include *Playboy Enterprises, Inc. v. Welles*, 60 F. Supp. 2d 1050 (S.D. Cal. 1999) and *Murphy Oil USA, Inc. v. Fluor Daniel, Inc.*, 52 Red.R.Serv.3d 168 (2002 WL 246439 (E.D.La).

Numerous confidentiality issues arise in connection with the use of e-mails. There are many stories about e-mail being accidentally sent to the wrong recipient. Correctly distributed e-mail is often easily forwarded with the click of a button to people never anticipated by the originator. A supervisor ends up with a forwarded copy of a disgruntled employee's e-mail to other employees, for example. Or in the context of litigation between parties, someone inadvertently forwards a copy of an internal e-mail to counsel for the opposing party.

At a minimum, when sending e-mail that you believe contains confidential or privileged information intended only for the eyes of the recipient, it is wise to include a confidentiality and privilege notice with the message, as well as a statement requesting that if someone other than the intended recipient receives it they are to advise you of the error and destroy the message. An example of such a notice is as follows:

> This e-mail/telefax message and any documents accompanying this transmission contain ATTORNEY-CLIENT PRIVILEGED INFORMATION and ATTORNEY WORK PRODUCT. It is confidential information and is intended solely for the addressee(s) named above. If you are not the intended addressee/recipient, you are hereby notified that any use of, disclosure, copying, distribution, or reliance on the contents of this e-mail/telefax is strictly prohibited and may result in legal action against you. Please reply to the sender advising of the error in transmission and immediately delete/destroy the message and any accompanying documents. Thank you.

When sending e-mail, we need to be mindful of who may gain access to the message and any attached documents. We also need to be aware that when the message is deleted from the e-mail folders of the sender and receiver, it may still exist on e-mail servers and computers elsewhere, as well as on backup disks or tapes. We have learned from recent case law, such as the two cases cited above, that parties to litigation are required to provide their electronic documentation to counsel for the opposing party, and to maintain and preserve such documentation just as they would paper documentation. The electronic documentation must also be presented in a usable manner. In the *Fluor* case, the court stated that computer back-up tapes containing e-mails would have to be reformatted at the cost of the party that made them, so they could be read by the other party.

A number of courts have issued adverse sanctions against parties for deleting electronic documents that were subject to discovery in litigation. If you are creating a document retention policy, it should address maintenance and retention of electronic documentation (including e-mail) just as it does paper records.

Chapter 5

The Purpose of Design and Construction Contracts

By: *Ava J. Abramowitz, Esq., Hon. AIA*

There are high stakes in contract negotiation, and those stakes do not revolve merely around insurability and fee. On the contrary, negotiating a contract is the last, best, relatively low-stakes opportunity that architects and their clients have to align themselves for project success–whether that client is the owner or a contractor. While the terms you negotiate will vary depending on your client, the contract is still the time to align the parties for project success. However, for the purposes of this discussion, I will assume throughout the book that your client is the owner.

Why "low-stakes opportunity"? Should negotiations fail, all you have to lose is the commission (assuming you have not started project delivery without a contract). Not your reputation due to a project gone awry. Not your insurance deductible because of a claim. Not unpaid services for lack of a contract. Indeed, you just may find yourself much better off for losing that project.

Accordingly, for you as an architect, a contract should never be just about negotiating words or coming to "yes" about legal terms. Rather, a contract serves many purposes, every one of which is in your interests and can be made to serve you, the owner, and the project. Let's take them one by one:

- *At its most basic, a contract makes the progress of the project predictable.* It is the "legal schematic" that describes how the project will go if it proceeds well, or if it does not. This view of a contract as a legal schematic is true for every party to the building enterprise, not just for you. So all parties benefit from a contract that defines the construction process. That fact will empower you throughout the negotiation because you can use it as a tool to negotiate project-friendly terms.

- *More broadly, a contract helps the parties achieve their strategic objectives.* Architects, perhaps due to their schooling, don't always understand this. They believe owners retain them to design a building, and, if the building is well designed and, later, the construction is well administered, they have done a good job. Not so. That is not enough for most of today's owners. As one owner said to me, "Architects don't get it. To them, the project stops when it is built. To me, it is still going on. I need a building as a tool to help me solve a problem. Design is never my goal unto itself." Contract negotiation affords the owner the opportunity to lay out his or her strategic goals, as well as giving you the chance to lay out yours. It gives you both the chance to understand each other and decide whether you really want and can work together. Again, as we will see in the next chapters, this realization can empower you during the negotiation process.

- *A contract affords both parties the opportunity to set realistic expectations of the other.* In order to be an effective tool that allows a project to be predictable, a contract must be grounded in realistic expectations. Negotiation is the time to work out project scope, budget, roles, quality, quantities, and timing. Now is the time for both parties to discuss and understand the implications of what they can and cannot do.

- *A well-negotiated contract assigns an exposure to the party in the best position to manage the risk, and then gives that party all the responsibility and power he or she needs to handle the exposure successfully, including fee.* Intuitively, this makes sense. There is no sound reason to assign an exposure to someone not capable of handling it, or to give anyone insufficient resources to manage a risk. Project success doesn't result from hedging. Nor does design excellence. Claims do. Contract negotiations provide the parties the chance to align scope, strategy, systems, and budget to enhance the possibilities of success.

- *Contracts can provide the framework that can facilitate future negotiations.* Because the owner and architect continue to negotiate the design of the project after the contract is signed, negotiation doesn't end with the initial contract. It is an ongoing process throughout the project. Many neophytes in design and construction, including nonconstruction lawyers, don't understand that once a contract is signed, an entirely new series of negotiations begins, from what the design should look like to how it should be configured. And let us not forget change orders, which become a fact of life as the owner sees the building for the first time and gets a better sense of what he or she really wants. A contract with too tight an intellectual framework can disadvantage the parties, no matter what the project. A framework that is too loose can be just as problematic.

- *Contracts help solidify the working relations the parties will need to succeed.* In addition to securing implementable language, contracts help secure working relationships. Expert negotiators leave the table with three things: (1) an agreement similarly understood by both parties; (2) an agreement that can be successfully implemented; and, (3) a willingness by the other party to negotiate with them again. Design contracts need all three of these attributes secured, as design and construction will inevitably involve continuing negotiations. If a contract is fought too hard or adversarially, a troubled project is probably not far behind.

- *Contracts are a private law—a law written by two parties that our public courts will enforce.* I put this purpose of contracts at the end because it is the least important of all the purposes of contracts for one reason and one reason alone: most projects succeed. It is the rare project indeed that ends up in court or even becomes the object of litigation. But when a contract does land in court, it is invariably enforced.

Though it is true that most projects succeed, that's never a reason for negotiating a sloppy or unimplementable contract. Doing that just increases your chances that your contract will be one of the few that ends up in court. Nor should you use the fact that insurers estimate that some 95 percent of the projects in America will go claims-free to assuage yourself into signing what you believe is an unconscionable contract. Courts are in power to enforce legal contracts. They look for ways to enforce contracts, to give the parties the benefit of their private law. They may agree that you were dumb to sign an egregiously one-sided contract, but in America, if you are competent to sign a contract, you have a legal right to sign a dumb one, and enforce it the courts will.

* * *

Four Key Concepts. How do these four concepts – exposure, capability, responsibility, and power – work together to facilitate contracts negotiation? You will see this more fully in later chapters [*Architect's Essentials of*

Contract Negotiation], but here is a précis. When you read a contract, ask yourself, paragraph by paragraph, section by section:

- What is the exposure inherent in the duty I am being asked to take on? Is it one I want to accept?

- Who is the person most capable of taking on the exposure? Is it me? Am I capable of handling it by myself now? If not, what do I have to do to make myself capable of managing the risk?

- Who has (or should have) the responsibility for managing the exposure? If it's me, are the duties laid out in the contract clear and sufficient enough for me to manage the exposure? Do I need more responsibilities? Which ones?

- Who has the power to make sure each responsibility is carried out effectively? If it's me, do I have enough authority to pull off those responsibilities? Enough fee? Will my authorities be correctly included in other parties' contracts?

Once you think through those issues, your negotiations will no longer focus on words and what's best for you versus what's best for the owner. Rather, you will be in the position to negotiate every aspect of the contract, including fee, from the vantage of *what's best for the project.*

In helping the owner think through what's best for the project, you will find yourself increasingly urging the owner to assign each exposure to the person most capable of managing the risk and then giving that person all the responsibility and power he or she needs to pull that exposure off. Sometimes that analysis will dictate that a new consultant be brought on the design team. Sometimes it will mean a construction budget is increased or a decreased in scope. Whatever it means, the bottom line is that the more thoroughly an exposure is thought through and planned for, the greater the chance of a successfully implemented project.

Analyzing contract clauses this way also gives you a greater opportunity for building your client's trust. Clients will see you thinking every issue through, not from your own self-interest, but from the vantage point of "what's best for the project." And, I ask you, what more can an owner negotiating in good faith want?[1]

---

[1] *Architect's Essentials of Contract Negotiation*, Ava J. Abramowitz, John Wiley & Sons, 1992, pp. 67-74. Editor's Note: This discussion was written by Ava J. Abramowitz, former deputy general counsel of The American Institute of Architects, and published in her book, *Architect's Essentials of Contract Negotiation*. I felt that I could not address this issue as well as Ava has done in her fine book, and so we reprint here, with permission, several pages of her text. Her book challenged my own thinking, as I'm sure it will challenge yours. If you follow her reasoning, you will find yourself asking more questions to help focus on your client's problems and needs, and you will learn to listen to them better so that you will propose solutions that go beyond their design needs and reach their basic business and personal concerns. All of us who learn to apply the principles of communication and negotiation so artfully and enjoyably explained by Ava, will better appreciate that we negotiate every day over little (and sometimes big) matters. Ava encourages us to approach negotiation from a new perspective instead of the tired old concepts of hard and soft negotiation, win-lose negotiation, or even win-win negotiation. Negotiation, as she explains, does not fit into simple formulas; it does not have to be complex; and it certainly does not need to be intimidating or dreaded. Whether you negotiate contracts with clients or just haggle with your boss, employees, or co-workers over every-day decisions in the office or in the field, this book is must reading.

Chapter 6

Contract Essentials

6.1	The Wisdom of Getting it in Writing
6.2	Basic Elements of the Professional Services Agreement
6.2.1	Scope of Services
6.2.2	Performance Schedule
6.2.3	Fee Schedule
6.2.4	General Terms and Conditions
6.3	Available Contracts Forms
6.3.1	Standard Form Agreements
6.3.2	AIA Documents
6.3.3	EJCDC Documents
6.3.4	DBIA Documents
6.3.5	Forms Created by Individual Design Professional Firms

6.1 The Wisdom of Getting it in Writing

Although parties may enter into legally binding contracts that are oral and never reduced to writing, it is wise to put professional services agreements in writing to the greatest extent possible. Design firms virtually always acknowledge that they seek to have a written contract for all services, but that they don't always get them.

The reasons for beginning work without a signed contract vary. Sometimes, an existing client gives a small project to a firm on a fast turn-around and no one thinks to get a written agreement since the parties are familiar with one another and understand the basic billing rates and procedures. Sometimes a contract is not executed because the services begin before the details of the contract get worked out. By the time the parties realize that they cannot agree upon the terms and conditions, the work is too far underway to stop, and the proposed terms are too onerous to accept in writing.

When the parties work without a written contract and there is a dispute over what the parties agreed to, the courts may look to correspondence and draft contracts that were sent back and forth. They might also consider oral evidence to decipher the parties' intent. Without a written contract, there is obviously more room for ambiguity, confusion, and disagreement, which leads to a greater necessity to have courts and arbitrators sort out the mess.

At a bare minimum, even if a written agreement is not being executed, the parties should get a written statement of the scope of services and the fee agreement. Getting the scope and fee established in writing is one of the most critical elements of the contract. It will avoid some of the greatest ambiguities and misunderstandings that typically result in disagreement and litigation.

A written contract has the added benefit of guiding the parties in their early communication with one another so that they better understand the expectations each has for the project. Contract negotiation should not be viewed as just a legal necessity. Instead, it should be seen as the beginning of the communication process that will help the parties understand each other and their needs throughout the project.

Failure to communicate during the contract negotiation and formation process will make it all the more difficult to communicate effectively during project performance. Good communication is the beginning and the end of effective risk management.

6.2 Basic Elements of the Professional Services Agreement

The key elements of any design professional agreement or contract include: (1) scope of service, (2) performance schedule, (3) fee schedule, and (4) the general terms and conditions.

6.2.1 Scope of Service

Services may be described in the basic agreement or as an attachment to the agreement. Under the American Institute of Architects (AIA) B141-1997, the services of the Architect are enumerated in Article 1.4. It is important that this article be filled in with some detail. If the Architect will also be performing Contract Administration Services, the terms and conditions of Article 2 of B141 will apply to those services. Section 2.8.2 of the AIA Agreement describes the contract administration services that will be provided. Additional services that may be provided for an additional fee are set forth in 2.8.3. This section provides a list of 22 additional items, which can be expanded or contracted as appropriate for the project. Under the Engineers Joint Contract Documents Committee (EJCDC) Document, EJCDC E-500 (2002), the Scope of Services is specified in Attachment A to the document.

Whether using an AIA agreement, EJCDC agreement, or some other form, the contract will generally identify basic services to be performed for an agreed upon fee, and additional services that can be performed for an additional fee if authorized in advance in writing by the owner. It's important that project managers for the design firm are careful not to perform "additional" services without first giving the owner notice, as required by contract, and obtaining authorization to perform these services for an additional fee. Otherwise, you may be unable to recover compensation for these services.

6.2.2 Performance Schedule

While negotiating the Agreement, it is important that the parties address expectations for the project schedule and come to agreement on what is reasonable. Unless the client's expectations are realistic, and the schedule agreed to by the design professional is feasible (taking into consideration the time that is needed to plan and design within the reasonable standard of care), there are going to be problems with a dissatisfied project owner.

Project owners who establish unrealistic schedules make bad matters worse when they require the design professional to be absolutely liable (pursuant to a "time is of the essence" clause) for completion of design services by specified dates. By doing this, they attempt to limit or even prohibit time extensions for excusable delays and may seek to hold the design firm responsible for construction delays beyond the control of the firm.

If a design firm agrees by the terms of its contract to assume liability for schedule delays, it may have an uninsured loss. The errors and omissions policy will only cover losses caused by the negligence of the firm. It will not respond to costs that arise out of warranties or guarantees to meet schedule deadlines.

By agreeing unconditionally to meet a specified schedule, the design firm may put undue pressure on itself to perform services quickly and without the generally accepted thoroughness and care—thereby increasing the risk of making an error.

If a contract establishes specific performance periods for the design professional to meet, it should also require the project owner to meet specified time periods for making necessary decisions and responding to requests from the design professional. Moreover, a provision should be included to clearly state that the design professional is not responsible for delays caused by others or delays that are not within its control.

6.2.3 Fee Schedule

Compensation for the design firm should be clearly established. In AIA B141-1997, this is done at Section 1.5.1. If the services change, or if additional services are added, there must be a simple way to calculate the revised fee. Section 1.5.2 of AIA B141 does this as follows: "If the services of the Architect are changed . . . , the Architect's compensation shall be adjusted. Such adjustment shall be calculated as described below . . . ." The parties are then advised by the AIA document to insert immediately following this last quoted sentence a basis of compensation, "including rates and multiples of Direct Personnel Expense for Principals and employees . . . ." Reimbursable expenses are also described and set forth in Article 1.5. These provisions provide a reasonable mechanism for the parties to accommodate changes to the project and services that are rendered.

It is important that the design firm not lock itself into a fixed fee (and reimbursable expense) that cannot be adjusted to reflect project changes in costs and time. In addition to the compensation clauses, the agreement should include a provision stating that the failure of the client to pay the consultant within a specified number of days from being invoiced will entitle the design firm to suspend or terminate its services until payment is made.

When design professionals get too far ahead of their client with services that have not been paid for, and then later try to catch up with their billing and payment, it is not uncommon to hear excuses from the client for why the design professional is not entitled to the full amount due. This may lead to the design professional filing a claim against its client to collect the balance of fees it believes is due. Such fee claims seem to inevitably result in the project owner defending itself by alleging that the design professional is not entitled to the fee because it performed its services negligently.

Moreover, as long as the client is defending itself against paying the additional fee, it is rather common for the client to counter-sue to recover from the design professional damages for change order costs it paid to the contractor and any other costs the owner asserts were caused by negligent performance. Prompt billing of the client by the design professional, and prompt action by the design professional to collect what is due when it is due, are two of the surest ways to manage risk. It is far better to argue over the fee today than to litigate over it tomorrow.

The design professional who is too shy to assert its right to a fee during its performance of services is a bad risk to itself and the insurance carrier. The insurance carrier may end up in the position of defending against claims that only came up because the design professional filed an affirmative claim for fee after the job was already complete.

6.2.4 General Terms and Conditions

General terms and conditions should not be overlooked by a contract reviewer as merely "boilerplate." In reality, these are vital terms of the contract that should not be glossed over by the parties and should not be assumed by the parties to be of no consequence. It is often in these clauses that the most significant risk is allocated. This is particularly true when the parties alter these terms and conditions by amendments (or interlineations) to the Agreement.

With the advent of electronic versions of the standard form agreements, it has become much easier to amend them. AIA and EJCDC require changes in the standard language to be indicated for easy identification. There may also be an addendum containing modifications to the printed terms which you should be sure to study carefully before signing the contract.

When asking your insurance advisor or attorney to review contract language, it is advisable to give them the entire contract and not just the clauses you want reviewed. If, for example, you gave your attorney only the insurance and indemnification clauses of a contract to review, he might miss the fact that numerous other sections of the contract also contain indemnification provisions or standards of care, warranties, and guarantees that are not insurable.

6.3 Available Contract Forms

6.3.1 Standard Form Agreements

Obtaining reasonable terms and conditions in contract documents is one of the most vital elements of risk management for the design professional and other parties to a construction project. The age old question is: "What is reasonable?" Some would argue that just as beauty is in the eye of the beholder, an opinion concerning whether contract language is reasonable will depend upon which party to the contract you ask. For this reason, contracts drafted by project owners may tend to favor the owner by allocating or shifting risk to the design professional or contractor. Likewise, contracts drafted by individual design professional firms may have a tendency to favor the designer.

In contrast, professional associations such as the American Institute of Architects (AIA), Engineer's Joint Contract Documents Committee (EJCDC), and the Associated General Contractors of America (AGC) have endeavored to produce standard form contracts acceptable to all parties to the agreement. In drafting these contracts, multiple entities and associations with an interest in construction have been consulted and given their input in creating documents that strive to maintain a reasonable allocation of risk. Reasonable risk allocation occurs when the contract allocates responsibilities and risks to the party in the best legal and practical position to manage the risk through its own actions.

One goal of the associations is to encourage the various project participants to use standard form agreements to the greatest extent possible, even if this means adding an addendum revising a few of the terms and conditions to accommodate the requirements of particular firms and their insurance carriers. Using standard forms goes a long way toward eliminating confusion and ambiguity over the intent and application of the language. After a contract clause has been interpreted and applied in different fact situations by courts around the country, parties using the form in the future have a pretty good idea of what the language means and what they are agreeing to when they sign such a standard form agreement. Using such contracts can save time during contract negotiation and give greater certainty to the outcome of potential claim issues that might arise under the contract.

Because various parties to the agreements bring their own agenda to the table, it is not uncommon to see supplements and addenda to these forms that reallocate the risk between the parties—different from what was intended by the standard form. When reviewing the agreements, it is critical that the parties focus on these addenda with their various revisions. If you are having an attorney review the agreement, it is particularly important to provide him with the entire agreement, including all the revisions.

6.3.2 AIA Documents

Suzanne Harness, Esq., AIA[2]
American Institute Of Architects

In 1857, The American Institute of Architects ("AIA") was founded by 29 architects meeting in New York City. The group shared the goal of creating an organization that would "promote the scientific and practical perfection of its members." Today the AIA is headquartered in Washington, DC and consists of more than 70,000 members with chapters, called components, in more than 300 locations.

One of the urgent needs the AIA addressed in the nineteenth century was the lack of any standardized contracting in the construction industry. Working with the Western Association of Architects, which later merged with the AIA, and the National Association of Builders, the AIA

---

[2] Suzanne Harness is Managing Director and Counsel, AIA Contract Documents, at the American Institute of Architects. As both a licensed architect and attorney, Suzanne's background includes construction law practice, owner representation in the private and public sectors, and architectural practice.

released its first standard form document in 1888. Called the Uniform Contract, this three page agreement between owner and contractor contained many concepts that were carried forward into the first General Conditions of the Contract, published in 1911. The successors to that 1911 document are published today as A201™–1997, General Conditions of the Contract for Construction. The AIA published its first owner/architect agreement in 1917.

Today, the AIA publishes nearly 100 standard form documents for use in the design and construction industry. These documents include agreements to create contracts for design or construction, construction management and design-build; general conditions documents to establish the terms and conditions of the contract; instructions to bidders; qualification statements for architects and contractors; bonding forms; payment and change order forms; a Request for Information form; and a number of forms used in managing the design or construction project. These standard forms may be used as-is, modified only to insert project-specific information, or may be edited further to change the standard text, on the agreement of the parties. AIA Contract Documents are available in paper format, or electronically in AIA Contract Documents software.

Documents are revised generally on a ten year cycle to accommodate changes in practice and to respond to any relevant judicial decisions affecting the interpretation of the document. As of this date, the AIA Documents Committee is already well underway in preparing revisions to the A201™–1997, General Conditions of the Contract for Construction for the 2007 edition.

The AIA intends to ensure that its documents, to the fullest possible extent, fairly represent the interests of those significantly affected by a particular document. The AIA also intends that its agreements avoid unreasonable bias by first allocating risks and responsibilities to the party with the most knowledge of the risk and in the best position to control it, next to the party best able to protect against unexpected cost, as for example, by the purchase of insurance, and then to the owner, as the ultimate beneficiary of the project, only when no other party can control the risk or prevent the loss.

AIA documents are organized by family and by series. A family of documents is a type of classification that refers to the type of project or project delivery method. AIA families of documents include: A201, or the Conventional; Small Projects, Construction Manager as Adviser; Construction Manager as Constructor; Interiors, International, and Design-Build. Documents are organized by series using a letter prefix to represent the type of agreement or document, as follows: A series - Owner/Contractor documents; B series - Owner/Architect documents; C series - Architect/Consultant documents; D series - industry documents, and G series - Contract Administration and Project Management Forms.

In late 2004, the AIA released 12 new contract documents, including a new Design-Build Family, six new architect's scope of services documents, and a Request for Information (RFI) form.

The 2004 Design-Build Family is not a simple update, but instead applies an entirely new approach to design-build delivery, replacing the two-part A191, A491, and B901 agreements of the 1985 and 1996 editions with one-part agreements, renumbered A141–2004, A142–2004, and B143–2004. In addition, the AIA has added two brand new documents, B142–2004, an agreement between the owner and a design-build consultant, and G704/DB–2004, a new form for acknowledging substantial completion of the design-build project.

In 1997, the AIA revised the format of B141, the AIA's foremost owner/architect agreement, by separating the agreement portion from the scope of services. The AIA made that change in recognition of the fact that many architects were not performing traditional design and construction services, and needed an agreement form that would allow the introduction of a specialized scope of services. In December 2004, the AIA introduced six new architect's scope of services documents for such specialized services. These include B204-2004, Value Analysis; B205-2004, Historic Preservation; B206-2004, Security Evaluation and Planning; B210-2004, Facility Support; B211-2004 Commissioning; and B214-2004, LEED® Certification. These are not standalone documents, but are to be used with B141-1997 to create an owner/architect agreement, or with G606-2000, Amendment to the Professional Services Agreement, to create a modification to any owner/architect agreement.

The AIA recognized that the practice of sending Requests for Information (RFIs) seemed to be creating as many problems as they solved. Contractors complained that due to inadequate contract documents they were compelled to generate numerous RFIs. Architects protested that contractors frequently requested information they could find easily in the contract documents. Taking these concerns into account the AIA published its first RFI form, G716-2004. Architects, owners, and contractors alike can use G716 to request information from each other. G716 asks the requesting party to list the relevant drawing, specification, or submittal reviewed in attempting to find the requested information.

Over the next few years, the AIA will issue additional scope of services documents, new agreements, and revisions to other document families. In each case, those revisions or new documents will reflect input received from industry and the changing practice of design and construction. In revising documents for 2007, the AIA is trying to anticipate how projects will be designed and delivered in 2017. For example, the three dimensional contract documents of the Building Information Model, which affect but a few projects today, could well be standard in less than ten years. It's clear that architects will need to change the way they deliver information to the contractor, and the contracts among the project participants will need to change as well. The AIA plans to ensure that its 2007 documents will address those concerns.

AIA Design-Build Documents

The AIA has created four contract documents to be used for design-build project delivery, as follows:

- AIA B142–2004, Standard Form of Agreement Between Owner and Consultant, establishes the contractual arrangement between an owner contemplating the design-build method of project delivery and the Consultant, who may or may not be an architect. Exhibit A to the Agreement provides the location for the parties to memorialize the initial information and assumptions upon which they base the agreement. Exhibit B to the Agreement provides an extensive menu of services from which the Owner and consultant may select.

- AIA B143–2004, Standard Form of Agreement Between Design-Builder and Architect, replaces B901–1996.

- AIA A141–2004, Standard Form of Agreement Between Owner and Design-Builder, replaces AIA A191–1996, and consists of the Agreement and three exhibits: Exhibit A, Terms and Conditions; Exhibit B, Determination of Cost of the Work; and Exhibit C, Insurance and Bonds. It forms the nucleus of the

Contract for Design-Build between the Owner and Design-Builder.

- AIA A142–2004, Standard Form of Agreement Between Design-Builder and Contractor, replaces AIA A491–1996 and consists of the Agreement portion and five exhibits. It forms the nucleus of the Contract for Construction between the Design-Builder and the Contractor.

6.3.4 Design Build Institute of America (DBIA) Documents

Michael C. Loulakis, Esq., Wickwire Gavin, P.C.[3]

The DBIA was founded in 1993 to respond to the challenges of an expanding design-build industry. It currently has almost 1,000 members representing the interests of owners, design-builders, and all others involved in the integrated design and construction process. One of DBIA's primary missions is the advocacy of best practices in the procurement and execution of design-build services, as well as the creation and dissemination of educational information on design-build.

The first DBIA contract document, DBIA 501 - Contract for Design-Build Consultant Services, was developed in 1996 and is intended to provide assistance to owners in the procurement and monitoring of design-build contracts. In 1997, the DBIA Manual of Practice Subcommittee began the process of developing model contract forms for the design-build team, with the publication of the DBIA *Design-Build*

---

[3] Mike Loulakis is President of and a Senior Shareholder in the law firm of Wickwire Gavin, where his practice concentrates on construction law. Mike was one of the principal drafters of the DBIA documents.

Contracting Guide ("Contracting Guide"). The *Contracting Guide* was used as a platform to establish DBIA's perspectives on best contracting practices and to compare such perspectives with those offered by the AIA, AGC, and EJCDC.

The principles expressed in the *Contracting Guide*, along with input received from the industry, made up the content for the DBIA design-build contract family. The first edition of DBIA's contract family consists of eleven documents. Four of these documents, issued in October 1998, relate to the relationship between the owner and the design-builder. They include:

- DBIA 520 - Standard Form of Preliminary Agreement Between Owner and Design-Builder

- DBIA 525 - Standard Form of Agreement Between Owner and Design-Builder - Lump Sum

- DBIA 530 - Standard Form of Agreement Between Owner and Design-Builder - Cost Plus Fee With an Option for a Guaranteed Maximum Price

- DBIA 535 - Standard Form of General Conditions Between Owner and Design-Builder

In October 1999, DBIA published its series of agreements between design-builder and subcontractors. These documents include:

- DBIA 540 - Standard Form of Agreement Between Design-Builder and Designer

- DBIA 550 - Standard Form of Agreement Between Design-Builder and General Contractor - Cost Plus Fee With an Option for a Guaranteed Maximum Price

- DBIA 555 - Standard Form of Agreement Between Design-Builder and General Contractor – Lump Sum

- DBIA 560 - Standard Form of Agreement Between Design-Builder and Design-Build Subcontractor - Cost Plus Fee With an Option for a Guaranteed Maximum Price

- DBIA 565 - Standard Form of Agreement Between Design-Builder and Design-Build Subcontractor - Lump Sum

Finally, in 2000, DBIA completed its contract family, releasing a contract between design-builder and trade subcontractor, DBIA 570 - Standard Form of Agreement Between Design-Builder and Subcontractor (Where Subcontractor Does Not Provide Design Services).

DBIA attempted to create a family of contract documents that was flexible enough to accommodate most design-build contracting arrangements. The DBIA forms anticipate that the design-builder executing the agreement could be: (a) an integrated design-build organization; (b) an organization led by a general contractor; (c) an organization led by a design professional, either an architect or an engineer; (d) a joint venture; or (e) a developer. This philosophy is evident by looking at the subcontract family. DBIA 540 (subcontract between design-builder and designer) is intended to be useful for those design-builders who are either developers or contractor-led organizations. In contrast, DBIA 550 and 555 (contracts between design-builder and general contractor) are intended to be used by designer-led design-builders or developers.

DBIA also recognized that the construction industry requires forms that are flexible enough to accommodate different contracting methodologies (i.e., lump sum, cost-plus, or guaranteed maximum price) and different procurement processes (i.e., competitive or negotiated). Hence, DBIA developed DBIA 520, a preliminary agreement which was intended to resemble Part 1 of AIA Document A191. DBIA 520 allows the owner to retain the design-builder for some preliminary services before agreeing to a complete design-build relationship. Owners may elect to use this document when they need a design-builder's assistance in developing project requirements and want to obtain a better understanding of the cost of performing the project.

This flexible view to procurement and contracting methodology is also reflected in the commercial contracts developed by DBIA. DBIA 525 is intended to be used when the design-builder will be paid on a lump sum basis. It is flexible enough for either a competitive or negotiated procurement system. DBIA 530 is to be used when the design-builder will be paid on a cost reimbursable basis and, while it is suitable for any procurement method, it was drafted with an assumption that it would be primarily used for negotiated selection because that is the more typical approach for cost-plus contracting.

Two other points should be noted about the DBIA standard forms. First, DBIA believed that it was important to directly address some of the more difficult contractual issues confronting owners and design-builders. These issues include the owner's right to use the design, payment for disputed change orders, obligation to correct design defects, and the design review process. In fact, DBIA's view on these major design-build issues has been instrumental in effecting changes in those forms developed by AIA, AGC, and EJCDC. Each of these organizations has used philosophies discussed in DBIA's *Contracting Guide* to modify its design-build approach.

Second, the DBIA documents are generally perceived as being well-balanced and fair, with special emphasis on protecting the owner's rights in the contracting process. This is particularly noticeable in the areas of owner's right to use documents and remedies for design defects.

6.3.6 Forms Created by Individual Design Professional Firms

Instead of using the standard forms of the AIA or other organizations (that require a royalty for use of the form), some firms choose to create and use their own forms. If you do this, it is highly recommended that you have your contract form reviewed by an attorney experienced with construction law in your jurisdiction and the locations where your project services will be performed.

You should also have the forms reviewed by insurance professionals such as brokers and insurance company personnel, who are familiar with the coverage available under the professional liability policy and how that coverage may be affected by the terms and conditions of your contract.

6.3.7 Forms Created by Project Owners

Contract forms created by project owners may establish risks for the design professional not covered by the professional liability policy. Examples include: (a) "highest standard of care," (b) indemnification for damages not caused by the negligence of the design professional, and (c) guarantees and warranties. Exercise extreme caution when executing a contract form that is prepared by the project owner. Get it reviewed by legal counsel and an insurance professional.

Chapter 7

Some Do's and Don'ts of Contract Language

7.1 Use Clear Language
7.2 Words to Avoid

7.1 Use Clear Language

Language that is imprecise, verbose, or unclear may create ambiguity and actually foil the efforts of the parties to communicate with each other. The parties' expectations may be confused and miscommunicated. As a result, the project and the principals may suffer.

Although it is important that the Agreement contain the basic legal requirements of a contract, it doesn't need to be written in legalese. Indeed, if it takes an attorney to understand and interpret the basic provisions of a contract, you can be pretty sure that it is not well written. When confronted during contract negotiation with language that is convoluted and confusing, don't be bashful about asking to have it clarified and revised into language that is simpler and more to the point. A good Agreement is one that can be understood by the project managers who need to understand their roles and responsibilities under that contract.

Be careful to review the Agreement to be sure that it does not scatter terms pertaining to the same matter into different sections of the contract. Contracts, for example, might include indemnification requirements in several different articles of the contract, addressing specific types of losses. In addition, the contracts may include an article titled "Indemnification" which is only general and applicable to issues not addressed by the more specific clauses. A contract might have a reasonable "Standard of Care" clause but also contain so much warranty and guarantee language elsewhere in the contract that the "Standard of Care" clause becomes meaningless.

It sometimes seems as if a project owner has intentionally done this to confuse the design professionals and their attorneys who might try to review the contract. Imagine if the design firm gave only the article entitled "Indemnification" to its attorney for review and then later discovered that the "Indemnification" article was fine, but was superseded by the more detailed and particular articles of the contract dealing with specific indemnification for property damage, bodily injury, and other causes.

7.2 Words to Avoid

Certain words create the impression that the design firm has a greater duty or responsibility than required by the generally accepted standard of care and scope of services stated elsewhere in the contract. Some words that risk managers often advise the design firm to avoid using in their contracts to the greatest extent possible include the following:

- "supervise contractor's work"
- "control contractor's work"
- "direct contractor's work"
- "guarantee or warrant either your services or the contractor's work"
- "certify that contractor's work meets the plans and specifications"
- "inspect contractor's work to assure it meets the plans and specifications."

Chapter 8

Marketing and Promotional Materials

Statements and representations contained in promotional materials, such as brochures and websites, may potentially create warranties, guarantees, or promises of highest or expert services. Even the cover letters that transmit a proposal for services may create promises of meeting higher standards of care that go beyond what is stated in the Agreement itself, and which may create liability that is not insured under the professional liability policy.

Some agreements state that they incorporate various materials, including cover letters, proposals, and marketing materials. This makes it even more important that we be aware of what is contained in those incorporated materials. Even if the materials are not specifically incorporated by reference, project owners might persuade a court to believe that they relied upon such representations and information contained in those materials. Owners may also persuade a court to believe that the design firm made the representations with the intentions for the project owner to act in reliance upon them.

It is important, therefore, that the design firm not include guarantees or over-state representations in the cover letters and marketing materials. Including such things could potentially subject you to liability you did not agree to in the Agreement itself.

Chapter 9

Insurance

9.1 What is Covered by a Professional Liability Policy?
9.2 Indemnification Provisions Affecting Coverage
9.3 Who is Covered?

9.1 What is Covered by a Professional Liability Policy?

Professional liability insurance is intended to cover negligent acts, errors, and omissions in the performance of professional services. Breaches of warranty and contract are not covered—except to the extent the breaches result from negligent acts, errors, and omissions of the policy holder. Coverage for claims arising out of anything other than negligence in the performance of professional services is not covered. The Insuring Agreement of a typical policy[4] provides, in part, as follows:

> WE will pay on behalf of the INSURED all sums in excess of the Deductible noted in Item 6. of the Declarations that YOU are legally obligated to pay as DAMAGES because of CLAIMS first made against YOU during the POLICY PERIOD and reported to US during the POLICY PERIOD, or the

---

[4] The policy language quoted in this Section 9.1 is excerpted from the Arch Insurance Group, Design Professional Liability Policy, copyright 2002 & 2003.

> Extended CLAIMS Reporting Period if applicable, provided that:
>
> *** the CLAIM arises out of an actual or alleged WRONGFUL ACT with respect to PROFESSIONAL SERVICES rendered or that should have been rendered by YOU or any entity for whom YOU are legally responsible, including YOUR interest in joint ventures.

Damages is defined by this policy as follows:

> DAMAGES means the monetary amounts for which YOU may be held legally liable, including sums paid as judgments, awards, or settlements, but does not include:
>
> 1. the restitution, return, withdrawal or reduction of fees, profits or charges for services rendered or offered or any other consideration or expenses paid to YOU or by YOU for services or products; or
>
> 2. judgments or awards deemed uninsurable by law.

And the policy defines Wrongful Acts and Professional Services as follows:

> WRONGFUL ACT means any negligent act, error or omission committed by YOU in the performance of YOUR PROFESSIONAL SERVICES.
>
> PROFESSIONAL SERVICES means those services that YOU are legally qualified to perform for others in YOUR capacity as an architect, engineer, designer, planner, land surveyor, or construction manager.

Insurance **69**

Certain costs or losses that you may incur may be excluded from coverage pursuant to either the policy definition of "damages", "Wrongful Act," or to one or more exclusions to the policy.

Key exclusions in the policy include the exclusion for express warranties and guarantees and also the exclusion for contractual liability.

Contractual liability is liability that arises out the terms and conditions of the contract that the design professional would not have under the law of the local jurisdiction in the absence of the contract language. For example, if the designer agrees to indemnify its client for all damages on the project regardless of whether caused by someone or something other than the negligence of the designer, this becomes a contractual obligation that exceeds the responsibility the courts would otherwise impose upon the designer. As explained in the "Standard of Care" discussion in the contract clause section of this Guide, courts don't impose liability on designers for every error, omission or mistake – but only those that are negligent because they fail to meet the standard of care. To the extent the contract imposes liability greater than this on the designer, the insurance policy will exclude that liability pursuant to the contractual liability exclusion of the policy.

A contractual liability exclusion of a typical professional liability policy provides as follows:

> This Policy does not apply to any DAMAGES, CLAIM or CLAIM EXPENSES based upon or arising out of:
>
> liability assumed by YOU under any oral or written contract or agreement, including but not limited to hold harmless and indemnity agreements,

agreements to defend others, and liquidated damages clauses, except that this exclusion shall not apply to a CLAIM where legal liability exists in the absence of such contract or agreement and arises from YOUR WRONGFUL ACT or the WRONGFUL ACT of YOUR subconsultants in the rendering of or failure to render PROFESSIONAL SERVICES;

The breach of warranty exclusion from the above-referenced policy provides as follows:

This policy does not apply to any DAMAGES, CLAIMS or CLAIM EXPENSES based upon or arising out of:

any express warranty or guarantee, except that this exclusion shall not apply to a CLAIM where legal liability exists in the absence of such warranty or guarantee and arises from YOUR WRONGFUL ACT or the WRONGFUL ACT of YOUR subconsultants in the rendering of or failure to render PROFESSIONAL SERVICES;

You should note that the above-quoted insurance policy language in this Section 9.1 is fairly typical of professional liability policies available today. The exact terms and conditions, however, will differ with each insurance company. For example, not all policies use the term "Wrongful Act." Regardless of what language is used, however, the intent is that the policy covers not every act and omission, but only those which are negligent. Throughout the discussions of contract clauses in Chapter 10 of this Guide, we discuss how the terms and conditions may impact the insurability of risks under policy language similar to that quoted above.

9.2 Indemnification Provisions Affecting Coverage

Indemnification provisions in contracts may require the design professional to indemnify, hold harmless, and defend its client against claims, damages, and allegations. If you agree to indemnify your client for anything other than damages arising out of your negligence in the performance of professional services, you will be contractually liable for damages that you would not have been liable for under "common law." To the extent that you incur losses due to contract language that is not due to the negligent performance of services, you have an uninsurable loss under the policy.

Insurance carriers and brokers routinely recommend that design professionals avoid agreeing to such an uninsurable indemnification obligation for this reason. There is an extensive discussion concerning the ramifications of indemnification provision in the contract clause example section of this Guide.

9.3 Who is Covered?

The professional liability policy is intended for the benefit of those who provide design professional services. This includes architects and engineers, and it may also include consultants, construction managers and general contractors, to the extent they are providing professional services for others. The Insuring Agreement quoted in Section 9.1 above provides coverage for:

> WRONGFUL ACT with respect to PROFESSIONAL SERVICES rendered or that should have been rendered by YOU or any entity for

whom YOU are legally responsible, including YOUR interest in joint ventures.

If a contractor is legally responsible for professional services provided under subcontract by a design professional, it may obtain a design professional policy to cover its legal liability. One benefit of a design professional policy is that it can cover purely economic losses even in the absence of property damage (PD) or bodily injury (BI). In contrast, a professional liability, errors and omissions (e&o) endorsement under a contractor's general liability policy provides only limited e&o coverage – typically limiting coverage to situations where PD or BI have also occurred.

Project owners have sometimes sought to be added as additional insureds to the design professional policy.

Chapter 10

Allocating Risks Through Contract Terms & Conditions

The goal when allocating the risk through the contract terms and conditions, as stated in earlier chapters, should be to allocate the risk to the party who has the best ability to manage that risk.

The contract can give ownership of the risk to any party. But if the party that accepts ownership of that risk does not also have the ability to manage that risk literally and legally, serious problems and legal consequences can be the result. Claims and litigation are more likely to occur on a project when a contract is grossly one-sided—shifting risks to a party that cannot reasonably manage those risks.

In the example clauses discussed below, the format is similar to one first used by this author in writing a contract guide for Zurich North America Insurance in the mid-1990s. This format is intended to provide a quick summary of issues and concerns arising out of various clauses, along with a discussion of some possible solutions. As will be reiterated throughout this Guide, the comments provided are intended only for insurance risk management educational purposes and are not intended as legal advice to be used in any specific situation or circumstance. In addition, permission to quote excerpts from standard form contracts of the AIA and EJCDC has been obtained, but in doing so, these excerpts may be taken out of context or may be incomplete and inappropriate for copying into an Agreement that you may be creating. Moreover, further use, copying, or reproducing of the clauses herein is not authorized by the AIA or EJCDC.

When negotiating any agreement for design professional services, it is advisable to obtain the assistance of legal counsel and insurance professionals knowledgeable with such contracts.

Allocating Risks Through Contract Terms & Conditions **75**

Contract Clause Examples

Notes/Comments: _____

Americans With Disabilities Act (ADA)

Issue: The Americans with Disabilities Act imposes liability upon the owner of a facility that designs and constructs it in a manner not meeting the accessibility and usability requirements of the ADA. An exception is made if it is structurally impractical to meet such requirements, but that becomes a factual determination often left to a jury to decide during a trial. The ADA also requires that if alterations to existing facilities are made, they must be readily accessible to individuals with disabilities to the maximum extent feasible.

Precisely what must be done to meet the ADA requirements is not clearly set forth in the law. It is necessary, therefore, for the project owner and design professionals to exercise reasonable care in forming their determinations (and professional opinions) as to what is required in the given circumstances of a project. Although the law appears to focus on project owners, it has also been applied against design firms and contractors who were found to have been in control of the design and construction of the facility. Courts in a few jurisdictions have imposed liability directly upon the design professional for failure to design to the ADA requirements. A number of other courts, however, have held that the ADA does not provide a statutory basis for claims against design professionals. Although this interpretation will prevent a group of disabled persons from suing the design professional directly, it will not necessarily protect design professionals from loss in the event the project owner is itself found in breach of the ADA and seeks indemnification from the design professional for its damages.

Discussion: In the clause below, the design professional is required to indemnify the project owner against any claim based on the violation of laws or codes—regardless of whether the designer met the standard of care:

> The Architect shall at all times observe and comply with all city, federal and state laws and regulations and shall defend the City ... against any claim or liability arising from or based on the violations of any law or regulation.

Even with the exercise of due care, it is possible that the professional opinion of the design firm concerning what is required by the ADA may differ from the opinion of someone working for the governing agency. Ordinarily, courts do not reverse a government agency unless it is proved that the agency acted arbitrarily, capriciously, or in violation of the law. That rarely happens. Consequently, if a project owner is required to pay fines and penalties, plus redesign a facility and pay to rip out and replace construction work, you may find yourself contractually liable to reimburse your client for all of these costs if you have signed a contract that committed you to strict compliance with the ADA or strict "compliance with all laws, ordinances, and regulations."

For the design professional, the insurance ramifications of such a contractual liability is that you may be denied coverage on the basis that the costs you pay to your client pursuant to your contractual obligation are not the result of damages caused by negligence in the performance of professional services. They may instead be found to be losses incurred as a result of a breach of warranty or guarantee. They may also be seen as arising out of "contractual liability."

Conclusion: Because of the uninsurable liability you will incur by agreeing to strict conformance with the ADA, it is more appropriate to negotiate the contract so it requires the exercise of the ordinary standard of care in complying with similar laws. This will give you a basis to defend yourself by proving that although you may have failed to comply with the ADA in the opinion of the government agency, and although fines, penalties, and damages may have been incurred by your client as a result, you are not legally liable if it can be demonstrated that you met the generally accepted standard of care in your efforts to comply with the law.

An example of applying the generally accepted standard of care to code compliance instead of committing to an absolute guarantee is exhibited in the following language:

> Consultant agrees that consistent with the standard of care applicable to this agreement it will identify, interpret and apply the design requirements of applicable laws, regulations and ordinances, including the Americans with Disabilities Act (ADA).

This clause is not intended for use without advice of counsel.

The AIA B141-1997 deals with code compliance in Section 1.2.3.6 as follows:

> The Architect shall review laws, codes, and regulations applicable to the Architect's services. The Architect shall respond in the design of the

> Project to requirements imposed by governmental authorities having jurisdiction over the Project.

This clause may not be reproduced without permission of AIA.

Note that by agreeing to "respond in the design" to the code requirements, it appears that the architect has agreed only to exercise the same standard of care in complying with the code requirements that it applies to all other aspects of its services.

The EJCDC Document E-500 (2002), at Section 6.01 E., provides for code compliance in such a way as to make compliance subject to the general performance standards set forth in the contract. It also goes a step further by protecting the engineer in the event that changes in the requirements become effective after the contract is executed. It provides as follows:

> Engineer and Owner shall comply with applicable Laws and Regulations and Owner-mandated standards that Owner has provided to Engineer in writing. This Agreement is based on these requirements as of its Effective Date. Changes to these requirements after the Effective Date of this Agreement may be the basis for modifications to Owner's responsibilities or to Engineer's scope of services, times of performance, and compensation.

This clause may not be reproduced without permission of EJCDC.

CAD and Electronic Media

Issue: Project owners are increasingly requesting (or demanding) that the design professional give them plans and drawings in electronic format because computer aided design and drafting has become the industry standard. Contracts drafted by owners are increasingly stating that ownership of and copyright to all Instruments of Services created by the design professional (including electronic data, files, plans, drawings, and specifications) are transferred by the design professional to the project owner. What problems arise out of giving the owner or others access to (or ownership of) the electronic documents?

Discussion: Due to the ease of making changes to electronic documents, there has been concern that owners and other entities might be able to manipulate and change the data for various purposes, including reuse on other projects or making subsequent modifications on the contracted project. If this happens, the design professional may be exposed to potential liability on each project where the documents are reused.

For electronic data to be transmitted accurately to the client from the design professional, a series of events is required including accurate transmission from the designer's computer and accurate receipt by a diskette, compact disk, and/or client's computer. It also requires compatibility between software programs maintained by the design professional and those who may be reading the documents on other computers.

For the basic fee for its services on a single project, the consultant might have risk of liability on multiple projects. In several recent contracts, major owner/developers that construct dozens of facilities per year have insisted on getting ownership of the design documents, with the right to reuse them on all of their projects. Despite the obvious dangers from both a risk management and business management perspective, design professionals have been willing to sign these contracts. At a minimum, you should protect yourself through indemnification and hold harmless provisions such as those referenced in the section of this course addressing ownership of documents.

Other problems with electronic data include the potential for data to become damaged or tainted during storage of diskettes or CDs. The shelf life of electronic media is relatively short and the data has a tendency to become unreadable or otherwise mixed up and unreliable over time. Relying upon such data several years after it has been stored could be risky. If a project owner or other party relies upon such data, it may suffer damages from defective design services resulting not from the original services but rather from subsequent decisions made in reliance on defective electronic media that has been stored and retrieved in a manner beyond your control.

Conclusion: To protect against these risks, maintain a hard copy set of final "Instruments of Service," such as plans and drawings. This will establish the benchmark against which to determine whether data in the electronic media are the same as in the final documents you produced.

It is important that the design professional be able to identify the source of information in the electronic documents and any changes that have been made to that documentation from what it originally provided as evidenced by the hardcopy drawings. The effectiveness of this evidence is enhanced by including in your contract with the owner terms and conditions to establish the hard copy

CAD and Electronic Media **83**

documents as the only documents to be relied upon. Example contract language providing some protection for the design professional against the potential misuse of its electronic documents is provided by the following:

> Consultant shall not be responsible for any alterations, modifications or additions made in the electronic data by the Client or any reuse of the electronic data by the Client or any other party for this project or any other project without the consent of the Consultant. Client shall defend, indemnify, and hold harmless Consultant against any claims, damages, or losses arising out of the reuse or distribution of the electronic data without consent of the Consultant and arising out of alterations, modifications, or additions to the electronic data made by anyone other than Consultant.
>
> Copies of Documents that may be relied upon by Client are limited to the printed copies (also known as hard copies) that are signed or sealed by the Consultant. Electronic text, data, graphics, or other files furnished by Consultant to Client are only for convenience of Consultant. Any conclusion or information obtained or derived from such electronic files will be at the user's sole risk.

This clause is not intended for use without advice of counsel.

Section 6.03 of EJCDC E-500 (2002) explains potential problems with the use of electronic media and provides the following:

B. ... Files in electronic media format of text, data, graphics, or other types that are furnished by one party to the other are furnished only for convenience, not reliance by the receiving party. Any conclusion or information obtained or derived from such electronic files will be at the user's sole risk. If there is a discrepancy between the electronic files and the hard copies, the hard copies govern.

C. Because data stored in electronic media format can deteriorate or be modified inadvertently or otherwise without authorization of the data's creator, the party receiving electronic files agrees that it will perform acceptance tests or procedures within 60 days, after which the receiving party shall be deemed to have accepted the data thus transferred. Any transmittal errors detected within the 60-day acceptance period will be corrected by the party delivering the electronic files.

D. When transferring documents in electronic media format, the transferring party makes no representations as to long-term compatibility, usability, or readability of such documents resulting from the use of software application packages, operating systems, or computer hardware differing from those used by the documents' creator.

This clause may not be reproduced without permission of EJCDC.

AIA B141-1997 states at Subparagraph 1.3.2.4 that before the Architect provides the Owner any documents in electronic format, a separate written agreement will be executed to set forth the conditions governing the format of the documents and establishing any special conditions on their use.

However you choose to address the issue of electronic documentation, try to minimize your potential risk from unauthorized use or reuse.

Certifications

Issue: Contract language requiring the design professional to certify that all work was completed by the contractor in conformance with the plans and specifications may create a guarantee or a strict standard of care that is not insured by the professional liability policy, since the liability may arise out of non-negligent performance of services. Design firm personnel are not constantly on the project site during construction. But even if such individuals were on the site, it is generally far beyond the scope of services for them to inspect or observe every detail of the contractor's work.

Discussion: It should be expected that a design professional will exercise the general standard of care in observing and monitoring the contractor's work, and that any certifications it signs will be consistent with that same standard of care. Design professionals should not be expected to go so far as to warrant or guarantee that which is certified.

A certification clause in one owner-generated contract requires the design firm to certify that "all work was performed by the contractor in accordance with all plans, specifications and contract documents." The owner could argue this created a strict assurance or guarantee by the design professional that the contractor met every design detail.

In a contract for land surveying services, an owner-generated contract required a "Surveyor's Certificate" that created an absolute warranty and guarantee that the surveyor had accurately reported information concerning the site in question—including information that was only available in public records such as easements and rights of way. It isn't reasonable for a surveyor to guarantee results—particularly with regard to information that it may only infer from its site observations and review of documents. Providing such a warranty would create an uninsurable risk for the surveyor since the professional liability policy covers only negligence in performance and not guarantees and warranties.

Conclusion: The contract itself should explain that the design firm will not be required to sign certificates attesting to anything about which it does not have personal knowledge. To the greatest extent possible, include a provision in the certificates stating they are based on your "knowledge, information, and belief," so that it is clear that you are stating a professional opinion and not providing a factual guarantee.

This is provided for at AIA B141-1997, Section 1.3.7.8, as follows:

> The Architect shall not be required to execute certificates that would require knowledge, services or responsibilities beyond the scope of this Agreement.

This clause may not be reproduced without permission of AIA.

Section 2.6.3.2 of AIA B141 states that the Architect's issuance of the payment certificate is not based on "exhaustive or continuous on-site inspections to check the quality or quantity of the Work...." This type of language is appropriate because it is consistent with the scope of services and the generally accepted standard of care. It is consistent with the real expectations of the parties as reflected by the Agreement.

Certifications

Section 6.01 F. of EJCDC E-500 (2002) prevents anyone from demanding that the design professional sign a certification based on anything other than actual personal knowledge of the conditions to which it certifies. This same clause also prevents the project owner from using financial leverage to force the design professional to sign such certifications. It provides as follows:

> Engineer shall not be required to sign any documents, no matter by whom requested, that would result in the Engineer having to certify, guarantee, or warrant the existence of conditions whose existence the Engineer cannot ascertain. Owner agrees not to make resolution of any dispute with the Engineer or payment of any amount due to the Engineer in any way contingent upon the Engineer signing any such documents.

This clause may not be reproduced without permission of EJCDC.

In the section of EJCDC E-500 (2002) that addresses certificates pertaining to completed construction work (Exhibit E, Notice of Acceptability of Work), the language places specific conditions upon the Engineer's determination that the contractor's work is acceptable. It states the following:

> 1. This Notice is given with the skill and care ordinarily used by members of the engineering profession practicing under similar conditions at the same time and in the same locality.
>
> 2. This Notice reflects and is an expression of the professional judgment of Engineer.

3. This Notice is given as to the best of Engineer's knowledge, information, and belief as of the date hereof.

4. This Notice is based entirely on and expressly limited by the scope of services Engineer has been employed by Owner to perform or furnish during construction of the Project (including observation of the Contractor's work) under Engineer's Agreement with Owner and under the Construction Contract referred to on the front side of this Notice, and applies only to facts that are within Engineer's knowledge or could reasonably have been ascertained by Engineer as a result of carrying out the responsibilities specifically assigned to Engineer under such Agreement and Construction Contract.

5. This Notice is not a guarantee or warranty of Contractor's performance under the Construction Contract referred to on the front side of this Notice, nor an assumption of responsibility for any failure of Contractor to furnish and perform the Work thereunder in accordance with the Contract Documents.

This clause may not be reproduced without permission of EJCDC.

The bottom line is that all a design firm can realistically do is exercise reasonable care to observe whether the contractor is in general conformance with the plans and specifications. Committing to more than that and executing a certification guaranteeing the quality of contractor's performance may subject the design professional to an uninsurable loss.

Changes in Design Professional's Services

Issue: Changes to the design professional's services may be required for a variety of reasons, including program changes by the client or budgetary constraints caused by construction costs. Appropriate contract language is needed to manage the change process, including authorization for changes and payment for the changed services.

Discussion: Within reason, the design professional may need the flexibility to perform services differing from those specifically identified in its scope of services. Contracts such as EJCDC E-500 provide this flexibility. There are limits, however, to what either the design professional or the project owner should be able to do in the way of services beyond those identified in the contract.

If contract language permits too much discretion to the owner to direct changes in services without the approval of the design firm, you may find yourself in the position of performing services that are beyond those that you normally accept as within your risk management protocol. It is even possible that these services could be of a type or nature that is not covered by your professional liability policy. In the clause below, for example, the project owner has unfettered prerogative to order more services and the design firm has no say in what changes it will perform:

> **Changes and Claims:** An Owner may make changes in the Services to be provided, including changes in specifications and/or drawings, omitting or adding work, changing the schedule, and such other changes as the Owner deems appropriate. To the extent that this results in an increase or decrease in the cost of the Agreement, an equitable

adjustment shall be made in accordance with the schedule of fees and costs included in the Agreement.

Several distinct issues regarding changes include: (1) Are the services different from the original scope of services? (2) If the services are different, is mutual agreement needed before the design professional performs them or can a unilateral decision be made? (3) How are the changed services to be documented and will the owner pay for them?

Unless the contract clearly defines the scope of services and includes appropriate language limiting how changes to that specified scope can accomplished, there may be a tendency to see what is sometimes called "scope creep" as the services gradually grow beyond the original expectations without any formal revision to the contract.

Numerous disputes between owners and design professionals have resulted because the design professional performed services beyond those covered by the "basic fee" without first obtaining written authorization to include those services as "additional services" for which the design professional would be paid an additional fee.

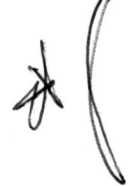

Such disputes can be avoided, or at least reduced, by plainly communicating the scope and change expectations of the parties in the contract language and then paying attention to the details of the contractual requirements before proceeding with changes in the services.

Conclusion: Negotiate a clause in your contract similar to that provided at AIA B141-1997, Section 1.3.3.1, which provides:

Changes in Design Professional's Services

1.3.3.1 Change in Services of the Architect ... may be accomplished ... if mutually agreed in writing, if required by circumstances beyond the Architect's control, or if the Architect's services are affected as described in Subparagraph 1.3.3.2..... Except for a change due to the fault of the Architect, Change in Services of the Architect shall entitle the Architect to an adjustment in compensation pursuant to Paragraph 1.5.2, ...

1.3.3.2 If any of the following circumstances affect the Architect's services for the Project, the Architect shall be entitled to an appropriate adjustment in the Architect's schedule and compensation:

.1 change in the instructions or approvals given by the Owner that necessitate revisions in Instruments of Service;

.2 enactment or revision of codes, laws or regulations or official interpretations which necessitate changes to previously prepared Instruments of Service;

.3 decisions of the Owner not rendered in a timely manner;

.4 significant change in the Project including, but not limited to, size, quality, complexity, the Owner's schedule or budget, or procurement method;

.5 failure of performance on the part of the Owner or the Owner's consultants or contractors;

.6 preparation for and attendance at a public hearing, a dispute resolution proceeding or a legal proceeding except where the Architect is party thereto;

> .7 change in the information contained in Article 1.1.

<small>This clause may not be reproduced without permission of AIA.</small>

The above provision requires that there be mutual agreement between the parties concerning the Changed Services. It also provides for compensation to the Architect. This becomes particularly important in light of what appears to be a push by project owners to require design firms to perform additional services at no cost to the owner—even when they result from design changes necessitated by construction changes or construction cost overruns not within the control or responsibility of the design professional.

Notice requirements may be included in one or more other provisions of the contract dictating that before the design firm may perform "additional services" it must first provide written notice to a designated representative of the owner and obtain written authorization for the changes, including agreement upon an additional fee. This provides appropriate protection for the project owner against an unwanted surprise invoice for services that the design professional thinks are "additional" but which the owner believed were always included within the original scope and "basic fee."

By learning in advance that the design professional intends to invoice for an additional fee for the changes, the owner might choose not to make the changes.

Where a firm performs additional services without following the notice and authorization provisions of the contract, the owner may assert that the design firm has waived any right to additional compensation. A number of courts have held that an owner is not required to pay a firm for services that were performed without proper notice and authorization—with the result being that the owner obtains essentially free services.

Notice requirements, including any time limitations on filing notice of change and documentation of costs, are to be taken seriously. So serious is this matter, in fact, that project principals and managers should be well trained in the terms and conditions of the contract applicable to these requirements, and internal systems should be put in place to assure that the requirements are being met.

Section A2.01 A.3 of EJCDC E-500 (2002) provides for compensating the engineer for additional services that result from various changes in the project and construction work beyond the engineer's control, including:

> Services resulting from significant changes in the scope, extent, or character of the portions of the Project designed or specified by Engineer or its design requirements including, but not limited to, changes in size, complexity, Owner's schedule, character of construction, or method of financing; and revising previously accepted studies, reports, Drawings, Specifications, or Contract Documents when such revisions are required by changes in Laws and Regulations enacted subsequent to the Effective Date of this Agreement or are due to any other causes beyond Engineer's control.

This clause may not be reproduced without permission of EJCDC.

The EJCDC E-500, at Section A2.02 A.3, also provides for compensation to the engineer for additional services resulting from changes due to material cost escalation. It provides for payment for *Additional Services Not Requiring Owner's Written Authorization*, including "Services resulting from significant delays, changes, or price increases occurring as a direct or indirect result of materials, equipment, or energy shortages."

Change Orders for Construction Work

Issue: It is becoming increasingly common to see contracts in which project owners require design professionals to take responsibility for construction cost overruns—even overruns that don't result from negligent performance by the design professional. Some owners are requiring design firms to assume financial responsibility for costs of change orders exceeding the contingency amount set aside for changes. If you contractually obligate yourself to pay these costs, your loss will not be covered by your professional liability policy unless the overruns are actually caused by your negligence.

Discussion: A fundamental point owners need to understand and accept is that performance of professional design services is an inexact art rather than an exact science. The owner should expect you to perform within the generally accepted standard of care; it should not expect perfection. If you were to create perfect plans, specifications, and documents, it would obviously take much longer, be much more expensive, and seriously impact the owner's ability to get the job done. In addition, it would possibly result in over-design with oversized structural members, redundant systems, and gold-plated designs, all costing the client more during construction.

Even assuming that perfection is possible, owners wouldn't be willing to pay for what it takes to achieve such perfection. Projects are designed and constructed with the understanding that some design changes will be necessary as the work progresses and that contractors will be paid under change orders for the extra costs they incur as a result of the design changes.

Over and over again it must be emphasized that on virtually every project there are design errors and omissions that do not cause legal liability for the design firm. There may be design errors and omissions that must be corrected—with the owner paying the contractor for its associated costs—yet the design firm will not be required by common law to reimburse the owner for those costs unless they rise to the level of being *negligent* errors and omissions.

By requiring the design firm to pay for construction changes not arising out of negligence, the owner makes an end run around the legal precedents applicable to design professional liability. The owner may even get around the standard of care clause in the contract that would have otherwise limited the design professional's responsibility for such change order costs. For coverage purposes, it's important for the design professional and owner to understand that these costs are subject to the contractual liability exclusion of the professional liability policy.

Some changes in construction are necessitated by material escalation costs. As this book is being written, the cost of steel is rising dramatically. Contractors are seeking to recover their increased costs of steel from owners. Design firms that are contractually required to redesign (without cost) to revise the project to meet a construction cost budget, or that are required to pay part of the change order costs, may be penalized for circumstances and changes beyond their control, unless the contract provides an exception for changes caused by material cost increases.

Another problem for the design professional who agrees to take responsibility for change order costs is that this may create a vested interest in the design professional to deny change order requests. This would be contrary to the duty of the design professional to act as an independent decision maker on the merits of change order requests. Contractors have filed law suits against designers, alleging that the rejection of their change order request by the designer was caused by the designer's fraud, misrepresentation, and conflict of interest.

In the clause below, the design professional assumes responsibility for making revisions to the construction documents as a result of a contractor's request for information, as part of its "basic services"—meaning without additional fee.

> *The Architect will produce a sufficiently complete set of Construction Documents so that a prudent and competent contractor can undertake and complete the Project with only minimal clarification from the Architect and without change orders. To the extent that a prudent contractor is unable to do so due to either insufficient information and/or ambiguities in the Construction Documents, the Architect will take whatever steps are necessary ... promptly to provide sufficient information and/or clarify ambiguities.... Such remedial actions on the part of the Architect will be undertaken as a part of Basic Services but such actions shall not serve to limit the Owner's remedies available under this Agreement or applicable law.*

In another contract, the owner takes an even more aggressive approach to recover costs associated with inaccuracies or discrepancies in the documents, thereby eliminating any defense the consultant may have available to it if the discrepancies are within the standard of care:

> *The consultant agrees to report promptly any inaccuracies or discrepancies, of all drawings and other information furnished to Contractor. Consultant agrees to accept responsibility for and*

pay any associated costs resulting from inaccuracies or discrepancies appearing in the drawings and other information furnished to Contractor, whether said inaccuracies or discrepancies are due to Consultant's work or from consultants hired by Consultant.

What clauses like these do is make the design firm responsible for the implied warranty of design owed by the owner to the contractor. At common law, the owner alone has that duty to the contractor and the designer owes no such duty. But by this contract language, the owner gives the designer full responsibility for costs owed the contractor under the owner's implied warranty even if the discrepancies were not negligent ones.

Conclusion: Before signing a contract, be sure you've discussed with the owner the likely need for change orders during construction, and the fact that some clarifications and changes in design will be necessary. It is important that clients appreciate that they are not getting perfect plans and specifications, and that there will be a need for changes in the plans as problems are encountered in the field during construction, and that they must share reasonably in this risk.

Contractors are entitled to recover for changes if they relied upon the accuracy of the plans and specifications during bidding. There is an implied warranty of specifications from the owner to the contractor. In contrast, the design firm does not give the owner or the contractor any express or implied warranty of specifications. This means that the owner may have to pay the contractor for changes but not be able to recover its costs for those changes from the design professional, even when the changes were necessary because of errors or omissions by the design firm. It is only when the errors and omissions arise out of the

Change Orders for Construction Work 101

design firm's negligence that the owner may recover its increased costs from the design firm. The contract language between the owner and design professional needs to reflect this.

Rather than design to perfection, it is generally understood that it is more cost-effective and efficient to get started with a design based on generally accepted standards, and make changes, as necessary, during construction by way of change orders and construction change directives to the contractor. The AIA B141-1997 deals with this briefly at Paragraph 2.6.5.2 "Changes in Work." In particular, it places the responsibility on the contractor to act responsibly and timely in seeking information and clarification. It provides the following:

> The Architect shall review properly prepared, timely requests by the Owner or Contractor for changes in the Work, including adjustments to the Contract Sum or Contract Time. A properly prepared request for a change in the Work shall be accompanied by sufficient supporting data and information to permit the Architect to make a reasonable determination without extensive investigation or preparation of additional drawings or specifications. . . .

This clause may not be reproduced without permission of AIA.

Changed Conditions
(Differing Site Conditions)

Issue: When conditions are discovered at the site during construction that are different from those represented by the contract (called a Type I differing site condition) or from those reasonably foreseeable by the contractor for the location where the work is being performed (called a Type II differing site condition), the contractor is generally entitled to receive a change order for an equitable adjustment in price and/or time. To the extent these differing site conditions (DSCs) cause the design professional to have to perform additional services or incur additional time and expense, the owner should be expected to make an equitable adjustment to the design professional accordingly. This may include both time and money.

Discussion: An increasingly persistent problem today is that project owners are listening to bad advice and barring DSC claims by contractors and design professionals. They are including clauses in their construction contracts stating that the bidder/contractor is responsible for doing its own site investigation and may not rely upon any information or site data provided by the client.

Some project owners are also including "no damage for delay" clauses stating that if the work is delayed for any reason, the most that the contractor can obtain in the way of equitable adjustment is additional time but no money. These provisions make for adversarial working relationships between the parties and do not enhance project cooperation.

Project owners have been encouraging their design professionals to draft similarly onerous language for construction contracts and then manage the construction contracts for the owner in a harsh and unreasonable manner. When this occurs, the design professional makes itself the adversary of the contractor. Sometimes, the design professional just needs to tell the owner that the project will go better if the owner treats the parties with respect and writes contract language accordingly.

Denying the contractor changes for differing site conditions may force him to turn normal DSC claims into claims alleging design flaw and negligence on the part of the design professional. Contractors don't generally give up their effort to be paid an equitable adjustment merely because a contract clause denies them a change order for DSCs. They will often file suit against the project owner and even the design firm, alleging everything from interference with their work, inadequate coordination by the owner, and misrepresentation to fraud, breach of contract, and negligence. Instead of dealing with a simple DSC, the design professional and owner may find themselves litigating endlessly over allegations that could have been avoided if the contract had been drafted in an appropriate fashion from the beginning.

Conclusion: The design professional should recommend that the project owner include a differing site condition clause in the construction contract and permit the bidders to reasonably rely upon data and information provided by the owner during the bidding process. This would eliminate the need for the contractor to include contingencies in its bid for any unknown conditions it might encounter and for which it might not be paid.

The design professional should also get language in its own contract to compensate it for additional time and costs incurred as a result of the contractor or design professional

Changed Conditions (DSCs)   **105**

encountering differing conditions. A sample clause is as follows:

> Client and Consultant agree that the discovery of unanticipated, changed conditions may require a renegotiation of the scope of services or a termination of services. Client shall rely on Consultant's judgment as to the continued adequacy of this Agreement in light of discoveries that were not anticipated or known. If Consultant determines that renegotiation is necessary, Consultant and Client shall in good faith enter into renegotiation of this Agreement to permit Consultant to continue to meet Client's needs. If renegotiated terms cannot be agreed to, Client agrees that Consultant has the right to terminate this Agreement. If the Agreement is terminated, Client shall pay Consultant for all services conducted and expenses incurred up to and including the date of termination.

This clause may not be reproduced without advice of counsel.

Another contract example providing the design professional with compensation for the impact DSCs have on its work is presented in the following clause. This clause also addresses environmental assessments the consultant might perform as a result of the discovery of unknown conditions.

> Site Access and Conditions
>
> Unless otherwise agreed in Attachment A, the Client will furnish the Consultant with any right of access

to the site necessary to provide the Services. If unexpected site conditions or other contingencies develop as the work is in progress, the Consultant will perform additional services with prior authorization from the Client and will provide written confirmation of any additional costs. All costs incurred because of unexpected site conditions, including any delays in authorizing the additional services, will be billed to the Client in addition to the charges authorized in Attachment B. The Consultant's performance of environmental assessments and project surveys are based on site conditions existing at the time the site visit/inspection occurs.

This clause may not be reproduced without advice of counsel.

Choice of Law & Venue

Issue: More than one jurisdiction could have authority to resolve disputes arising under your contract. If you are a Delaware corporation performing services on a project in Florida, for example, it is possible that courts in either state could have jurisdiction over a claim. If you, a Delaware corporation, enter into a contract with an owner that is incorporated in Texas, but you are providing services for a project being constructed in Florida, it is possible that courts in all three states could be called upon to resolve disputes between you and the project owner. The jurisdiction where a dispute is resolved is called the "venue."

The parties may choose to apply the law of any of the jurisdictions that could have venue, even if the matter is not decided in that particular jurisdiction. Thus, the dispute could be tried in the courts of Florida where the project is located, but with the court applying the requirements of Delaware laws to its decisions.

Discussion: Some states of incorporation have laws more favorable to corporations than other states. Indemnity and limitations of liability provisions in contracts, for example, may be enforceable under the laws of one state but found contrary to public policy or statutes in another state. If you are incorporated in a state with favorable laws, you may find it beneficial to have those laws applied to your contracts wherever they are performed. The attorneys who regularly assist you with contracts and disputes will be better able to provide assistance as you negotiate contracts in other jurisdictions if you are able to apply the law of your own jurisdiction—particularly if you are able to require disputes to be resolved in your own jurisdiction.

Conclusion: Include clauses in the contract specifying which state that will have jurisdiction and which state's laws will apply to the contract. An example of such a clause is the following:

> If a dispute arises over the meaning, interpretation or operation of any term, condition, definition or provision of this contract, it is agreed that the substantive law of the State of New York shall apply regardless of the choice of law or conflicts of law principles.

This clause is not intended for use without advice of counsel.

Another example is:

> The construction, validity and performance of this Agreement shall be governed by and construed under the laws of the state of _____, and for all matters arising under, out of, or in connection with this Agreement, the parties shall submit to the exclusive jurisdiction of the courts of the said state.

This clause is not intended for use without advice of counsel.

EJCDC E-500, Section 6.06(A), provides as follows:

> This Agreement is to be governed by the law of the state in which the Project is located.

This clause may not be reproduced without permission of EJCDC.

Choice of Law & Venue **109**

In contrast, AIA B141, Section 1.3.7.1, provides:

> This Agreement shall be governed by the law of the principal place of business of the Architect, unless otherwise provided in Paragraph 1.4.2.

This clause may not be reproduced without permission of AIA.

Compliance with Law

Issue: In performing professional services, design professionals are required by common law to meet the generally accepted standard of care. This includes exercising reasonable care to comply with applicable laws, ordinances, and regulations. Some project owners are, by their contract language, imposing stricter compliance requirements—essentially getting an unconditional guarantee that the design professional will perform services in strict conformance with all laws and regulations. Some contracts go so far as to require strict conformance to not only those laws and codes in effect as of the date of the contract execution, but even those that are issued or changed during the performance of the services—and without additional compensation. An example of a clause imposing what amounts to a guarantee is the following:

> *The Architect shall review laws, codes, and regulations applicable to the Architect's services. Architect shall cause all drawings, specifications, documents and other Work required to be performed by Architect to be prepared in accordance with all federal, state, and local statutes and regulations governing the Project and the Work, it being specifically understood that Architect shall be responsible for interpreting applicable regulations so that all aspects of the facility may be utilized for the purposes intended.... Should Architect fail to comply with Legal Requirements, or fail to produce a design that complies with Legal Requirements, Architect hereby agrees to bear all resulting costs.*

This clause creates a guarantee or warranty that the design professional will meet all laws, codes, ordinances, and regulations, and that if it is determined that its design does not conform to all such requirements, the Architect shall bear the resulting costs—apparently without regard to whether the design professional performed in a manner consistent with the Standard of Care.

Discussion: Instead of promising absolute compliance, agree to exercise the generally accepted standard of care to comply with the applicable laws and codes. If you incur a loss to your client because you didn't meet the strict guarantee of code compliance but your failure to comply didn't result from negligence, you will have no coverage available for that loss. This is because coverage would be excluded under one or more policy exclusions, including the exclusions for warranties, guarantees, and contractual liability.

Problems with this are abundant. First, the question of what is specifically required by laws, ordinances, codes, and regulations is a very subjective one. What one person reasonably believes is necessary may not be what another person (and, in particular, a government agency employee) may deem to be required.

By agreeing to comply with all laws, you are imposing upon yourself a duty to research and determine every arcane law that might apply. By agreeing to strict adherence to the laws, you may be agreeing to reimburse your client for any fines, penalties, or re-design and re-work costs resulting from a government decision concerning the interpretation of the law that is different from how you interpreted the same law.

By agreeing to "comply with all laws, ordinances and regulations," a design professional may be deemed to have warranted strict compliance. Despite the exercise of due care, it is possible that the professional opinion of the design firm may differ from what someone working for the governing agency may deem to be required.

Generally speaking, courts are deferential to the determinations and opinions of government agencies when it comes to interpreting their own laws and regulations. This means that even if your interpretation was reasonable, a court could conclude that the government agency is entitled to assess penalties against your client, the project owner, based upon your failure to meet the more strict interpretation of the law applied by the government agency.

Courts don't ordinarily reverse a government agency unless it is proved that the agency acted arbitrarily, capriciously, or in violation of the law. That rarely happens. Consequently, if a project owner is required to pay fines and penalties, plus redesign a facility and pay to rip out and replace construction work, you may find yourself contractually liable to reimburse your client for all of the costs if you have signed a contract that committed you to strict compliance with the law.

The insurance ramifications for the design professional are that coverage for these costs may be denied on the basis that they are not the result of damages caused by negligence in the performance of professional services. They may instead be found to be losses incurred as a result of a breach of warranty or guarantee. They may also be seen as arising out of "contractual liability." All such costs are excluded as damages under the professional liability policy.

Conclusion: Because of the uninsurable liability you will incur by agreeing to strict conformance with the law, it is appropriate to negotiate your contract so it requires you to exercise the ordinary standard of care in complying with laws. This will give you a basis to defend yourself by proving that although you may have failed to comply with the laws in the opinion of the government agency, and although fines, penalties, and damages may have been incurred by your client as a result, you are not legally liable. That is so if it can be demonstrated that you met the generally accepted standard of care in your efforts to comply with the law. An example of a clause by which only the generally accepted standard of care has been agreed to is as follows:

> Consultant shall exercise the generally accepted standard of care to render professional services in compliance with applicable laws, ordinances, and regulations.

This clause is not intended for use without advice of counsel.

This next clause avoids a warranty situation by expressly limiting the design professional to the generally accepted standard of care. It also eliminates responsibility for changes in the law after contract execution:

> In performing professional services, Consultant shall exercise the generally accepted standard of care in the identification and interpretation of applicable codes, laws, regulations, and standards. Changes in Laws and Regulations after the execution of this Agreement that were not known or reasonably foreseeable affecting the cost or time of performance may be the subject of a change order.

This clause is not intended for use without advice of counsel.

The AIA B141-1997, Section 1.2.3.6, establishes the responsibility within the ordinary standard of care for how the Architect will be performing all of its services. It provides as follows:

> The Architect shall review laws, codes, and regulations applicable to the Architect's services. The Architect shall respond in the design of the Project to requirements imposed by governmental authorities having jurisdiction over the Project.

This clause may not be reproduced without permission of AIA.

In summary, explain to your client that it is not realistic to expect you to identify, interpret, and apply every conceivable law, regulation, and ordinance in precisely the manner that the governing agency or some other party believes it should be applied.

If your client incurs damages because of your incorrect interpretation and application of a law or regulation, you need to be able to defend yourself by presenting expert testimony to show that your interpretation was not negligent—even if it was incorrect. If your interpretation was wrong, but not negligent, your policy will not cover you if you have contractually obligated yourself to pay for your client's damages regardless of fault.

Legal Question: Is Code Compliance Failure a Contract or Tort Claim?

A court applied a three-year statute of limitations for negligence claims to dismiss a claim against an architect for code compliance failure. The plaintiff asserted that a six-year period for breach of contract claims should be applied, not the shorter period for negligence actions. The court held that the essence of the claim was that the architect had negligently performed its contractual services, and the legislative intent was if a claim arises out of professional negligence, the shorter limitations period applies. *Kliment & Frances Halsband. v. McKinsey & Company, Inc.*, 3 N.Y.3d 538 (Dec. 2004).

At issue was whether a contract provision concerning code compliance constituted an express guarantee that elevated the architect's responsibility to higher than the normal standard of care. The contract provided the following: "All plans, drawings, specifications and other documents prepared by Architect or its consultants or engineers ... shall be in compliance with all laws, codes, ordinances and other requirements applicable to the Project (including without limitation the relevant building code....)."

The court concluded that while the architect expressly committed by contract to comply with code requirements, it did not provide an express warranty. Therefore, this was not a breach of contract claim and the requirements applicable to professional malpractice claims—such as the shorter statute of limitations period—were appropriate. Thus, the issue is whether the architect complied with the generally accepted standard of care. In a negligence-based action, a claimant must prove that the architect failed to comply with a code provision and that it was negligent in doing so. The court held, "Making such ordinary obligations express terms of an agreement does not remove the issue from the realm of negligence ... nor can it convert a malpractice action into a breach of contract action." The court's reasoning is quite important because many contracts seem to attempt to make the design professional contractually liable for any and all errors, regardless of negligence.

Confidentiality

Issue: An appropriately worded confidentiality clause in the contract will permit you as the design professional to share information concerning services with your subconsultants and with individuals other than your client, as required by law. Some project owners are drafting confidentiality clauses so strict that they would prevent the design professional from divulging information to anyone, including government agency personnel, despite the fact that the design professional is under legal obligation to do so. Consider the following clause:

> *The Architect agrees that all knowledge and information not already considered within the public domain which the Architect may acquire from the Owner by virtue of performing services hereunder, will be regarded as strictly confidential and held in confidence and shall not be disclosed to anyone without the Owner's prior written consent to such disclosure.*

This clause puts the design professional in the untenable position of having to breach its contract with its client in order to comply with the legal requirements of the law to disclose certain information.

Discussion: Information pertaining to public health and safety may be required to be reported pursuant to ethical obligations, such as those promulgated by the National Society of Professional Engineers (NSPE) Code of Ethics. The NSPE Code in turn has been incorporated into state licensing statutes in several states and the failure to comply with the Code could subject the Engineer to a violation of the state licensing law and result in censure or loss of license.

Some state environmental laws and regulations also impose an independent duty upon the design professional to report directly to the state agency about any knowledge it obtains during the performance of its services on land concerning any ongoing release of pollutants. For all these reasons, it is important not to agree to a confidentiality clause that is overly strict.

Conclusion: Negotiate a confidentiality clause that protects the client, but gives you the flexibility to report information as required by law. Consider the following clause:

> All data, documents, discussions or other information developed or received by or for City in performance of this Agreement are confidential and are not to be disclosed to any person except as authorized in writing by City, or as required by law.

This clause is not intended for use without advice of counsel.

The final phrase, "or as required by law," appears to give the design professional discretion to decide when information must be released. Some contracts make this more difficult by stating that the design professional may only release the information when required to do so by court order or subpoena. That is not acceptable because, in many cases, the duty to disclose is required by law even without a court order or subpoena, and the contract language needs to recognize that possibility.

Return to the example of the bad clause in the introduction to this discussion. One potential remedy would be to add a new phrase at the end of the paragraph stating, *"provided, however, that the information is not otherwise required to be disclosed by law, or in the opinion of the A/E required to assure the health or safety of the public."* In  negotiating this change to the contract, you would explain to your client that you cannot avoid your ethical or legal duty to disclose certain confidential information, and that you are sure the client would not want to put you in that position or put itself in the position of causing such a situation. If the client still is not comfortable with the explanation and the change, you might alleviate some of its concern by agreeing to add another sentence to the paragraph stating that when you are required to disclose information, you will first advise the client that you will be making the disclosure. At least this will protect it from surprise.

An example of a reasonable clause from a manuscript contract is as follows:

> Any confidential information, including proprietary information, exchanged between the Client and the Consultant in connection with this Agreement shall be kept confidential by the recipient, except to the extent that such information must be communicated (a) to third parties in connection with the performance of this Agreement; (b) as required by governmental agencies or otherwise required by law; (c) as required for financial, insurance or tax audits, subject to a confidentiality agreement with the auditor; or (d) as may be authorized in writing by he party from whom that information originated. This provision shall not apply in the event that the information is or becomes part of the public domain other than by breach of the parties, or was known to

> the other party prior to the making of the proposal for the Project. This obligation shall survive suspension, termination or expiration of this Agreement.

This clause is not intended for use without advice of counsel.

Another reasonable approach to confidentiality is presented by AIA B141–1997, Clause 1.2.3.4:

> The Architect shall maintain the confidentiality of information specifically designated as confidential by the Owner, unless withholding such information would violate the law, create the risk of significant harm to the public or prevent the Architect from establishing a claim or defense in an adjudicatory proceeding. The Architect shall require of the Architect's consultants similar agreements to maintain the confidentiality of information specifically designated as confidential by the Owner.

This clause may not be reproduced without permission of AIA.

Cost Estimates

Issue: In the event that construction bids or costs come in higher than the engineer's estimate, owners are more frequently requiring design professionals to assume the risk (and cost) of revising plans and specifications. In some contracts, owners are essentially demanding that design professionals warrant that the construction work will be completed for the estimated construction costs.

An example clause from an owner-generated contract is as follows:

> *As part of the Schematic Design Documents, the Consultant shall provide to the University a construction cost estimate . . . The Probable Construction Cost shall not exceed the Project Construction Cost. In the event that it does, the Consultant, without additional compensation, in conjunction with the Construction Manager and the University, shall re-design the Project as necessary to maintain the Project Construction Cost.*

Discussion: In the contract above, this was just the first of many clauses that would make the design professional responsible for all cost overruns regardless of whether there was negligence by the design professional. Other clauses required the design professional to prepare construction estimates and stated that any re-design needed to get the construction bids down to the estimate would be performed at the design professional's expense. If the cost model update submitted by the contractor during construction exceeded the project budget, the design professional contract required the following of the design professional:

> *If the Consultant is unable to effect cost reduction revisions in the Construction Documents without deviating from the design and intent of the previously approved documents, the Consultant shall ... await instructions which the University shall issue to the Consultant concerning future action to be taken under the Agreement. The instructions issued by the University at its sole discretion shall include redesign of the Project as necessary in conjunction with the Construction Manager and the University to meet the Project Construction Cost without additional compensation.*

Another example of a clause that puts the design firm in an unfavorable position with regard to cost overruns beyond its control is as follows:

> *In the event that the lowest responsive bid exceeds the Fixed Limit of Construction Cost, the Architect, if directed by Owner, shall redesign the Project with the assistance of the Construction Manager in order to bring the Project within budget. Architect shall not be entitled to additional compensation for this redesign or any services required for the re-bidding of the Project. The Architect shall be responsible for any and all costs incurred by the Owner which are attributable to the redesign or re-bidding of the Project.*

Some contracts make it clear that cost overruns are going to be taken out of the fee otherwise paid to the design firm. One contract states that the owner will hold back $10,000 to be used as damages in the event that the project does not come in on budget or there are any problems with the design professional's services. The design professional should understand that this money may never be released to it. It becomes too easy for the owner or Project Team to withhold the money and force the design professional to fight for it.

It is seldom worth fighting for withheld money. Practically every suit for withheld payment results in a counter-suit that the design professional regrets. Even when the design professional prevails, the legal fees often eat up the amount of the fee in dispute. It is important to note that costs related to fee disputes between project owners and design professionals are not covered by the professional liability policy.

Conclusion: Since the professional liability policy will not cover cost overruns that aren't the result of negligent performance of services, it is important that the client understand he's putting you into a position of paying costs out of your own limited assets, without the benefit of insurance coverage. You should not agree to language guaranteeing a cost estimate.

Because costs can escalate for any number of reasons unrelated to design acts or errors and omissions, there is no reasonable basis for a project owner to put this risk onto the design firm.

Instead of providing a "cost estimate" and committing to having the project constructed for that "estimate," it may be more prudent to use language stating that the design professional will provide only an "opinion of probable costs." By using this language, it is more obvious that you are offering a professional opinion conditioned upon ordinary due care, and this does not constitute a warranty or guarantee of costs. If the "opinion" proves to be incorrect and the owner makes a claim against you for damages, you will be able to defend yourself by presenting expert testimony to show that your opinion, although incorrect, complied with the generally accepted standard of care and you have no liability for negligence.

Contract clauses should clearly state the cost opinion or estimate is not a guarantee of cost either as to the consultant's fee or to the ultimate construction costs to be paid to others. An example is as follows:

> Consultant shall prepare an opinion of the probable costs of construction. Consultant has no control, however, over (a) the cost of labor, material, or equipment; (b) the means, methods and procedures of the contractor's work; or (c) the competitive bidding. Consultant's opinion of probable cost shall be based on its experience and qualifications and represent its judgment as a Consultant familiar with the construction industry but shall not be a guarantee that construction costs will not vary from its opinions of probable cost.

This clause is not intended for use without advice of counsel.

Section 5.01 of EJCDC E-500 (2002) provides as follows:

> Opinions of Probable Construction Cost
>
> Engineer's opinions of probable Construction Cost are to be made on the basis of Engineer's experience and qualifications and represent Engineer's best judgment as an experienced and qualified professional generally familiar with the construction industry. However, since Engineer has no control over the cost of labor, materials, equipment, or

Cost Estimates

services furnished by others, or over contractors' methods of determining prices, or over competitive bidding or market conditions, Engineer cannot and does not guarantee that proposals, bids, or actual Construction Cost will not vary from opinions of probable Construction Cost prepared by Engineer. If Owner wishes greater assurance as to probable Construction Cost, Owner shall employ an independent cost estimator as provided in Exhibit B.

_{This clause may not be reproduced without permission of EJCDC.}

Where the project owner requires the engineer to design within a specified budget, the EJCDC E-500, Exhibit F5.02, *Designing to Construction Cost Limit*, subparagraph F., provides a detailed mechanism for accomplishing this for the owner while at the same time protecting the engineer against uninsurable loss:

If the lowest bona fide proposal or Bid exceeds the established Construction Cost limit, Owner shall (1) give written approval to increase such Construction Cost limit, or (2) authorize negotiating or rebidding the Project within a reasonable time, or (3) cooperate in revising the Project's scope, extent, or character to the extent consistent with the Project's requirements and with sound engineering practices. In the case of (3), Engineer shall modify the Contract Documents as necessary to bring the Construction Cost within the Construction Cost Limit. Owner shall pay Engineer's cost to provide such modification services, including the costs of the services of Engineer's Consultants, all overhead expenses reasonably related thereto, and Reimbursable Expenses, but without profit to

> Engineer on account of such services. The providing of such services will be the limit of Engineer's responsibility in this regard and, having done so, Engineer shall be entitled to payment for services and expenses in accordance with this Agreement and will not otherwise be liable for damages attributable to the lowest bona fide proposal or Bid exceeding the established Construction Cost limit.

_{This clause may not be reproduced without permission of EJCDC.}

The EJCDC Document E-500, Exhibit A2.02 A.3, also provides that the engineer will be compensated for its additional services resulting from changes in the construction and price increases resulting from material escalation.

Damages

Issue: The typical design professional liability policy defines the "damages" that are covered by the policy. Certain types of losses that you may incur may be excluded from coverage pursuant to either the policy definition of "damages" or to one or more exclusions to the policy.

Discussion: The Damages that are covered by a professional liability policy of one carrier are defined as follows:

> *DAMAGES means the monetary amounts for which YOU may be held legally liable, including sums paid as judgments, awards, or settlements, but does not include:*
>
> *1. the restitution, return, withdrawal or reduction of fees, profits or charges for services rendered or offered or any other consideration or expenses paid to YOU or by YOU for services or products; or*
>
> *2. judgments or awards deemed uninsurable by law.*

The typical contractual liability exclusion of a design professional policy reads as follows:

> *This Policy does not apply to any DAMAGES, CLAIM or CLAIM EXPENSES based upon or arising out of: ... liability assumed by YOU under any oral or written contract or agreement, including but not limited to hold harmless and indemnity agreements, agreements to defend others, and liquidated damages clauses, except that this*

> *exclusion shall not apply to a CLAIM where legal liability exists in the absence of such contract or agreement and arises from YOUR WRONGFUL ACT or the WRONGFUL ACT of YOUR subconsultants in the rendering of Professional Services.*

If you accept a contractual obligation to pay liquidated damages to your client or to pay specific fines and penalties for which you are not liable at common law, you may incur an uninsured loss.

Conclusion: Some professional liability policies define damages differently than the policy quoted above. Instead of denying coverage for "judgments or award deemed uninsurable by law," the policy may deny coverage for fines, penalties, and punitive damages. This distinction could become important in determining whether you can recover under your policy for certain losses you may incur, such as those related to alleged violations of the Americans with Disabilities Act and Department of Labor OSHA standards.

Professional liability carriers intend for their policies to cover actual damages. They believe it is possible to evaluate actual damages in most cases involving alleged design error. Furthermore, they believe that liquidated damages are not appropriate for design professional contracts. The problem is that project owners who are used to including liquidated damages clauses in their construction contracts sometimes think that the same principles of recovery should apply to design firms. As you can see from the above-quoted contractual liability exclusion, however, if you agree to liquidated damages, the carrier may deny coverage pursuant to the contractual liability exclusion of the policy. This would be particularly problematic if the liquidated damages provision has been coupled with a delay clause whereby you agreed to pay liquidated damages for delay in the completion of your services. If the owner recovers against you by summary judgment on those contract provisions without having to prove your negligence or the actual damages, you may find yourself with a denial of coverage by the carrier.

When confronted with these types of clauses in contracts, you may be able to persuade your client that it is in its best interest as well as your own to delete such uninsurable provisions since it may defeat your client's ability to recover against you if your carrier is going to contest the coverage of these "damages."

liquidated damages

Dispute Resolution

Design professionals generally prefer not to think about disagreements turning into formal disputes requiring resolution by third parties. Insurance brokers, insurance companies, and lawyers who represent the design professionals, however, must review every contract and every communication between parties with a keen knowledge that the outcome of an eventual dispute may depend upon the wording of that contract, document, or communication. Although we may not want to dwell on disputes, it is helpful to the project management and risk management process to plan, execute, and document the services with the view that formal dispute resolution may one day be necessary on your project.

You should review several related issues in this book concerning disputes in order to get a more complete understanding of managing your risks to avoid disputes where possible and to facilitate the most effective and efficient dispute resolution when a dispute can't be avoided.

Several contract clauses, in addition to the disputes clause, can significantly impact dispute resolution. These include the "Choice of Law," "Time Limitations," "Limitation of Liability," "Indemnification," "Severability," and "Survival" clauses.

Issue 1: Reporting a Claim Against You

Your insurance policy specifically outlines what you will have to do in the event of a dispute—including timely notice to your insurance company, and making no decisions and taking no actions concerning a claim that would prejudice the rights and interests of the insurance company. The policy states your rights and obligations with regard to claim reporting and claim resolution. An example from a design professional policy is quoted below:

Notice of CLAIM

In the event of a CLAIM, YOU shall provide to US prompt written notice containing particulars sufficient to identify YOU or any INSURED involved and reasonably obtainable information with respect to time, place and circumstances, and the names and addresses of any injured parties and of available witnesses. YOU further agree to send US copies of all demands or legal documents as soon as possible.... All CLAIMS are to be reported to: [Insurance Company] [Insurance Company address].

No costs, charges or related CLAIM EXPENSES shall be incurred without OUR written consent which shall not be unreasonably withheld. WE shall have the right and the duty to designate legal counsel for the investigation, defense or settlement of a CLAIM. WE will not settle or compromise any CLAIM without YOUR consent. YOU shall do nothing to prejudice OUR rights under this Policy nor shall YOU admit liability or settle any CLAIM without OUR written consent. If YOU refuse to consent to any settlement or compromise recommended by US involving any part of OUR limits of liability and acceptable to the claimant, and YOU elect to contest the CLAIM, suit or proceeding, then OUR liability shall not exceed the amount which WE would have paid for DAMAGES and CLAIM EXPENSES at the time the CLAIM or suit or proceeding could have been settled or compromised.

YOU shall assist and cooperate with US in the investigation, settlement and defense of all CLAIMS made against YOU and upon OUR request shall authorize the release of records and other information, secure and give evidence, attend hearings and trials and obtain the location of and cooperation of witnesses. Any expenses YOU incur resulting from such cooperation are not considered CLAIMS EXPENSES, and are thus not recoverable under this Policy or chargeable against YOUR Deductible.

Discussion: Some important points to note from the above-quoted language are the following:

(1) You are to report the claim directly to the insurance company at the address indicated in the policy;

(2) You are not to incur claim defense costs without prior authorization of your insurance carrier;

(3) You are to do nothing to prejudice the rights of the insurance carrier, nor are you to settle the claim without the carrier's consent; and

(4) If you refuse to consent to any settlement or compromise recommended by the carrier and instead contest the claim, resulting in an award against you greater than what the carrier would have paid to settle the case, the carrier limits its liability to you to the amount it would have paid for the settlement.

This last clause is sometimes referred to as the "hammer clause," because the design professional may potentially get hammered if it forces a matter to trial that could have been settled for a lesser amount.

Note that the notice must go directly to the insurance carrier. Design firms often first informally talk to their insurance broker about a claim before submitting a formal notice of claim to the carrier. It is important to understand, however, that pursuant to the terms of the policy, the formal written notice is to go directly from you to the company and address stated in the policy.

Issue 2: Mediation

Disputes are increasingly being resolved through mediation. Mediation, however, can be a precursor to either arbitration or litigation. It produces a non-binding result and is basically a form of settlement discussion. The contract can set forth mediation or other alternative dispute resolution procedures to precede that final binding process. Of course, the mediation can produce a settlement that becomes binding once it is agreed upon by the parties and recorded into a binding agreement.

Mediation has been so efficient and cost-effective at resolving construction and design professional disputes that a number of insurance carriers have provided a credit to the deductible to encourage the use of mediation. As mediation has become the industry standard, however, a number of carriers have ceased offering this. You may want to consult your broker about the availability of such mediation credits.

On complex or lengthy projects, there may be distinct advantages to resolving disputes during the construction process rather than waiting until project completion. This is sometimes done through Dispute Resolution Boards that are established pursuant to terms of the contract.

It is important when establishing a dispute resolution process in the design professional agreement that the parties to the contract consider how disputes between others on the project will be resolved and whether all organizations, at every tier and subtier, will be included in a single dispute resolution if they have a stake in the outcome.

Discussion: Include language in the contracts between the owner and design professional, as well as between the owner and the contractors, requiring mediation as a condition precedent to either arbitrating or litigating claims. Specify that if mediation fails to resolve the dispute, the parties then are free to proceed with other binding dispute resolution, including arbitration or litigation—as set forth in the contract agreement.

An example of a mediation clause is the following from AIA B14–1997, as follows:

1.3.4.1 Any claim, dispute or other matter in question arising out of or related to this Agreement shall be subject to mediation as a condition precedent to arbitration or the institution of legal or equitable proceedings by either party. . . .

1.3.4.2 The Owner and Architect shall endeavor to resolve claims, disputes and other matters in question between them by mediation which, unless the parties mutually agree otherwise, shall be in accordance with the Construction Industry Mediation Rules of the American Arbitration Association currently in effect. . . .

1.3.5.1 Any claim, dispute or other matter in question arising out of or related to this Agreement

> shall be subject to arbitration. Prior to arbitration, the parties shall endeavor to resolve disputes by mediation in accordance with Paragraph 1.3.4.

This clause may not be reproduced without permission of AIA.

EJCDC E-500 (2002) similarly provides for a step process to dispute resolution, beginning with negotiation, and proceeding through mediation or arbitration. Section 6.08 A. provides:

> Owner and Engineer agree to negotiate all disputes between them in good faith for a period of 30 days from the date of notice prior to invoking the procedures of Exhibit H or other provisions of this Agreement, or exercising their rights under law.

Clause not to be reproduced or used without permission of EJCDC

An example from a manuscript contract is as follows:

> If a dispute arises out of or relates to this Agreement or its breach, and if the dispute cannot be settled through direct discussions, the parties agree that prior to the filing of any legal action, they will first endeavor to settle the dispute in an amicable manner by non-binding mediation, using a certified mediator or certified mediation service. Failure of the parties to resolve the dispute through mediation shall in no way remove the right of either party to pursue any legal action or recourse.

This clause is not intended for use without advice of counsel.

In the next clause, the parties have agreed to include mediation provisions in all agreements with other parties involved with the project. This will avoid the situation where a subcontractor or other party that may have an interest or even causation in the claim is left out of the mediation process and opts to go straight to court instead:

> In an effort to resolve any conflicts that arise, the Owner and Consultant agree that all disputes between them arising out of or relating to this contract or the Project shall be submitted to non-binding mediation unless the parties mutually agree otherwise. The Owner and Consultant further agree to include a similar mediation provision in all agreements with independent contractors and consultants retained for the Project and to require all independent contractors and consultants also to include a similar mediation provision in all agreements with their subcontractors, sub-consultants, suppliers and fabricators, thereby providing for mediation as the primary method for dispute resolution between the parties to all those agreements.

This clause is not intended for use without advice of counsel.

Issue 3: Arbitration

Issue: Although conventional wisdom has been that arbitration can be a more cost-effective and efficient means to resolve disputes than litigation, this is not always the case—particularly with complex construction disputes. With complex construction litigation, it is often beneficial to obtain full discovery of the facts through interrogatories and depositions of witnesses and experts. The abbreviated proceedings in arbitration may not permit the parties to adequately develop and prove their case. Moreover, it may render it difficult for an insurance company to determine the basis for an arbitration decision.

If an arbitration decision is rendered with no factual and legal explanation, and the claim was based on multiple theories of law such as negligence, breach of contract, and warranty, it may be impossible for the insurer to ascertain the basis for the arbitration award.

Some carriers may also be concerned that arbitration is not necessarily geared towards a fair allocation of liability based upon law and facts, but may instead "split the baby in the middle," thereby penalizing the design professional.

Discussion: If the contract calls for arbitration in the event a dispute is not successfully resolved by mediation, it is advisable to require that any arbitration award include a detailed decision containing findings of fact and conclusions of law. This is important so that an insurance carrier may determine from the face of the award decision the basis for the damages.

When arbitration is conducted over a period of many months with the arbitrators meeting only sporadically, it is difficult to understand how they can remember the details of the case and reach a decision as well reasoned as that of a court that conducts a full hearing at one time and place. In addition, with the limitations upon document discovery and testimony and cross examination, it can be more difficult to ascertain the genuine facts of the matter.

Another shortcoming of arbitration proceedings is the lack of Motions Practice that is available in court proceedings that permit parties to file motions for summary judgment and motions to dismiss. Whereas you might be entitled get out of a court case by filing a motion to dismiss based on the expiration of the time permitted by the statutes of limitations or statues of repose, you might not be able to use those same statutory time limitations to get dismissed out of arbitration proceedings.

Before entering into binding arbitration proceedings, be sure to discuss with your insurance broker and insurance carrier any requirements that the carrier may apply. It is entirely possible that your carrier may prefer litigation of a complex construction matter in order to obtain full discovery of the facts, including production of documents and witnesses for cross-examination. Moreover, on complex cases, it may be more efficient with regard to both time and cost to litigate rather than arbitrate.

The AIA B141–1997 provides as follows:

> 1.3.5.1 Any claim, dispute or other matter in question arising out of or related to this Agreement shall be subject to arbitration. Prior to arbitration, the parties shall endeavor to resolve disputes by mediation in accordance with Paragraph 1.3.4.
>
> 1.3.5.2 Claims, disputes and other matters in question between the parties that are not resolved by mediation shall be decided by arbitration which, unless the parties mutually agree otherwise, shall be in accordance with the Construction Industry Arbitration Rules of the American Arbitration Association currently in effect. The demand for arbitration shall be filed in writing with the other

> party to this Agreement and with the American Arbitration Association.

<small>Clause not to be reproduced or used without permission of AIA.</small>

A sample clause from a manuscript contract requiring arbitration decisions to include findings of fact and conclusions of law is the following:

> Any claim, dispute or other matter in question arising out of or related to this Agreement shall be subject to binding arbitration pursuant to the rules and procedures of the American Arbitration Association. The arbitrator or arbitration panel will be required to issue a decision that includes detailed findings of fact and conclusions of law, and any decision that fails to include such findings of fact and conclusions of law shall be null, void, and unenforceable.

<small>This clause is not intended for use without advice of counsel.</small>

Other Issues to Consider with Regard to Arbitration

If the contract contains a mandatory arbitration clause, consider revising it to make it a voluntary decision to be mutually agreed upon by both parties when a dispute arises. This can be done by substituting the word "may" for "shall" in the language stating that disputes "shall" be submitted to arbitration. This will permit the parties to make a more informed decision concerning whether arbitration or litigation is most appropriate for a particular dispute and in their best interest. If arbitration is decided upon at that later date, a more complete arbitration agreement can be agreed upon at that time, including terms such as requiring the arbitrators to issue a detailed decision with facts and law.

Instead of agreeing to arbitrate all disputes, you might revise the contract language to require arbitration only for those disputes less than a certain dollar amount, or only for certain issues such as fee disputes or copyright infringement allegations.

You may want to carefully consider any language stating that the prevailing party will recover its attorneys fees from the losing party. Legal fees of the prevailing party could exceed the amount of actual damages recovered by that same party. The prevailing party might prevail on only 10% of its demand amount. Will you be required to pay 100% of that party's attorneys fees when 90% of the claim is rejected? Consider eliminating the prevailing party language altogether, or perhaps in some way limiting the attorneys fees.

Issue 4: Joinder of Parties into a Single Dispute Resolution

It is important that all entities with a stake in a claim be made a part of any dispute resolution process, including arbitration or litigation.

Discussion: This is generally accomplished by including in every contract, at every tier, a joinder requirement such as that included in EJCDC E-500, Paragraph H6.09 A.5, which provides:

> If a Dispute in question between Owner and Engineer involves the work of a Contractor, subcontractor, or consultants to the Owner or Engineer (each a "Joinable Party"), either Owner or Engineer may join each Joinable Party as a party to

the arbitration between Owner and Engineer hereunder, and Engineer or Owner, as appropriate, shall include in each contract with each such Joinable Party a specific provision whereby such Joinable Party consents to being joined in an arbitration between Owner and Engineer involving the work of such Joinable Party. Nothing in this Paragraph H6.08.A.5 nor in the provision of such contract consenting to joinder shall create any claim, right, or cause of action in favor of the Joinable Party and against Owner or Engineer that does not otherwise exist.

Clause not to be reproduced or used without permission of EJCDC.

The AIA B141–1997 takes a somewhat different approach:

1.3.5.4. No arbitration arising out of or relating to this Agreement shall include, by consolidation or joinder or in any other manner, additional person or entity not a party to this Agreement, except by written consent containing a specific reference to this Agreement and signed by the Owner, Architect, and any other person or entity sought to be joined...

Clause may not be reproduced and used without permission of AIA.

Environmental Conditions

Issue: If addressing hazardous materials is not part of your scope of services, the contract can be written to specify who will be responsible in the event such conditions are discovered and what role, if any, the design professional or contractor will have.

Discussion: If your insurance program excludes coverage for pollution releases, you could incur an uninsurable loss if you perform services or work that cause a release of environmental materials.

Conclusion: Negotiate language into the Agreement that will protect you in the event that environmental conditions are encountered. An example of such a clause as follows:

> Consultant shall not arrange or otherwise dispose of Hazardous Substances under this Agreement. Consultant, at Owner's request, may assist Owner in identifying appropriate alternatives for off-site treatments, storage or disposal of the Hazardous Substances, but Consultant shall not make any independent determination relating to the selection of a treatment, storage or disposal facility.

This clause is not intended for use without advice of counsel.

This language has the effect of removing from the contractor much of the risk that might otherwise lead to strict liability under Superfund or other environmental statutes.

Another way to deal with this issue is along the lines presented by AIA Document B-141-1997, Section 1.3.7.6, which provides:

> Unless otherwise provided in this Agreement, the Architect and Architect's consultants shall have no responsibility for the discovery, presence, handling, removal or disposal of or exposure of persons to hazardous materials in any form at the Project site.

Clause may not be reproduced and used without permission of AIA.

One manuscript contract goes into great detail describing the matter as follows:

> **Unanticipated Hazardous Materials**
>
> The Client represents that, to the extent known to the Client, it has advised the Consultant of any hazardous waste or materials existing on or near the job site, including the identification of any hazardous substances, the extent or quantity, and the location thereof. In the event hazardous material is encountered by the Consultant during the course of performing its services, and if the Client did not advise the Consultant of the existence thereof, then the Client and the Consultant agree that the scope of services and schedule identified in Attachment A, and the cost estimates and compensation identified in Attachment B, shall be adjusted and compensation to the Consultant shall increase as is reasonably necessary. If the discovery of hazardous substances requires the Consultant to take immediate or emergency measures to protect health and safety or

prevent property damage, the Consultant agrees to notify the Client within a reasonable time following completion of such measures. Any adjustment in the scope of services and/or compensation shall include additional compensation for Consultant's implementation of emergency measures. The Client acknowledges that the Consultant has neither created nor contributed to the creation or existence of any hazardous, radioactive, toxic, irritant, pollutant, or otherwise dangerous substance or condition at the site. The Consultant's compensation hereunder is not commensurate with the potential risk of injury or loss that may be caused by exposures to such substances or conditions. Accordingly, in addition to any other indemnification provisions contained herein, the Client waives any claim against the Consultant and agrees to indemnify, defend and hold the Consultant, its officers, directors, agents and employees harmless from any claim, demand, liability or defense costs, including but not limited to attorneys fees and other incidental costs, for injury or loss alleged or sustained by any party which is based upon injury or damage caused by said hazardous material, except to the extent such claims arise out of the Consultant's own [gross] negligence or willful misconduct. The Consultant shall retain the right to participate in the defense to this Agreement or the Services performed hereunder, if the Consultant is named a party to such actions. The indemnity provisions herein shall survive termination or expiration of this Agreement.

This clause is not intended for use without advice of counsel.

Section 6.09 of EJCDC E-500 (2002, provides, in pertinent part, for the same issue in the following way:

> D. It is acknowledged by both parties that Engineer's scope of services does not include any services related to Constituents of Concern. If Engineer or any other party encounters an undisclosed Constituent of Concern, or if investigative or remedial action, or other professional services, are necessary with respect to disclosed or undisclosed Constituents of Concern, then Engineer may, at its option and without liability for consequential or any other damages, suspend performance of services on the portion of the Project affected thereby until Owner: (1) retains appropriate specialist consultant(s) or contractor(s) to identify and, as appropriate, abate, remediate, or remove the Constituents of Concern; and (2) warrants that the Site is in full compliance with applicable Laws and Regulations.
>
> E. If the presence at the Site of undisclosed Constituents of Concern adversely affects the performance of Engineer's services under this Agreement, then the Engineer shall have the option of (1) accepting an equitable adjustment in its compensation or in the time of completion, or both; or (2) terminating this Agreement for cause on 30 days notice.

Clause may not be reproduced and used without permission of EJCDC.

The EJCDC E-500 (2002) also addresses environmental issues by providing indemnification specially applicable to environmental liability. This is found at Section 6.10 C. as follows:

Environmental Indemnification. In addition to the indemnity provided under Paragraph 6.10.B of this Agreement, and to the fullest extent permitted by law, Owner shall indemnify and hold harmless Engineer and its officers, directors, partners, agents, employees, and Consultants from and against any and all claims, costs, losses, and damages (including but not limited to all fees and charges of engineers, architects, attorneys and other professionals, and all court, arbitration, or other dispute resolution costs) caused by, arising out of, relating to, or resulting from a Constituent of Concern at, on, or under the Site, provided that (i) any such claim, cost, loss, or damage is attributable to bodily injury, sickness, disease, or death, or to injury to or destruction of tangible property (other than the Work itself), including the loss of use resulting therefrom, and (ii) nothing in this paragraph shall obligate Owner to indemnify any individual or entity from and against the consequences of that individual's or entity's own negligence or willful misconduct.

Clause may not be reproduced and used without permission of EJCDC.

Incorporation by Reference

Issue: Some contracts contain a clause stating that another contract is incorporated by reference. For example, a design subconsultant's agreement might state that the terms and conditions of the prime architect's agreement with the project owner are incorporated by reference. In the context of a design-build project, a general contractor who is taking the lead role as the design-builder may flow down to its design firm subcontractor, by way of "incorporation by reference," the terms and conditions of the owner/contract agreement. A typical clause might read as follows:

> *The Subcontract Documents consist of (1) this Agreement; (2) the Prime Contract, consisting of the Agreement between the Owner and Contractor and the other Contract Documents enumerated therein; (3) Modifications issued subsequent to the execution of the Agreement between the Owner and Contractor, whether before or after the execution of this Agreement...*

Another example of incorporation by reference is as follows:

> *It is agreed that the terms and conditions of the contract between Owner and Client are hereby incorporated by reference into this agreement. All such terms and conditions are as fully binding upon the Design Professional as if set forth herein at length, to the same extent that Client is bound by the same to the Owner.*

Discussion: You might see clauses like these if you are providing services as a design professional subcontractor to a general contractor that is taking the lead on a design-build project. It is likely that the terms and conditions of the prime contract will be inconsistent with your own design professional contract with the client. By agreeing that your contract with the client will consist not only of the Agreement itself, but also the Prime Contract and any changes to that Prime Contract, you may inadvertently be agreeing to terms you do not know about in the prime contract. These terms might even supersede or override conflicting terms in your subconsulting agreement. It is possible, for example, that your client has agreed to a standard of care or indemnification requirement that is contrary to your own risk management principles. It is further possible that if those terms flow down into your contract and are enforced against you, you will incur an uninsurable loss.

Conclusion: Don't agree to incorporate by reference the terms of another contract unless you have read that contract and understand those terms. You need to assure yourself that the incorporated terms and conditions do not impose risk and liability on you different from what you are otherwise agreeing to in your Agreement with your client.

The AIA Standard Form of Agreement between Architect and Consultant (AIA C142–1997) provides the following incorporation by reference clause:

> A copy of the Architect's agreement with the Owner, known as the Prime Agreement (from which compensation amounts may be deleted), is attached as Exhibit A and is made a part of this Agreement.

Clause may not be reproduced and used without permission of AIA.

At least with the AIA language above, the prime agreement is to be attached to what you are executing so that you can review it.

If in reviewing the prime agreement language you find terms that conflict with the risk allocation provisions of your subcontract, you should seek to amend the above clause by adding an exception to incorporation for specific, identified articles of your subcontract.

To avoid confusion over the scope of services applicable to your subcontract that might arise from a general incorporation by reference of your client's prime contract, you may clarify your scope by specific reference and incorporation of the scope of service set forth in your own detailed proposal.

Indemnification

Issue: Indemnification provisions in contracts may require the design professional to indemnify, hold harmless, and defend its client against claims, damages, and allegations. If you agree to indemnify your client for anything other than damages arising out of your negligence in the performance of professional services, you will be contractually liable for damages that you would not have been liable for under "common law." In other words, the courts would not impose liability on you since you did not violate the standard of care, yet you may be found contractually liable irregardless of whether you were negligent, since that is what you agreed to by virtue of the contractual indemnification clause.

Indemnity clauses may include any, or all, of three distinct obligations, including to (1) indemnify, (2) defend, and (3) hold harmless the client. "Indemnify" means to reimburse your client following a loss. "Defend" means to pay the client's legal expenses as it defends itself against a third party claim. "Hold harmless" may have several meanings but most generally is understood to be your agreement to protect the client against harm from suits by either third parties or yourself.

If you agree to "defend" your client, you may incur your client's defense costs as it defends itself against a third party claim, and you may find that your insurance will not cover those costs. To the extent your obligation to pay these defense costs is based only on your contractual commitment and not common law, your carrier will likely assert that the contractual liability exclusion of the policy excludes these costs from coverage. This is important to remember. No matter how innocuous an indemnity clause may appear to you, if it requires you to "defend" the client for any reason, it may create uninsurable losses for you.

Discussion: A typical professional liability policy's contractual liability exclusion bars coverage for your contractually imposed obligation to "defend others." An example of such a clause is the following:

> *Contractual Liability.* This Policy does not apply to any damages, claims, or claim expenses based upon or arising out of liability assumed by You under any oral or written contract or agreement, including but not limited to hold harmless and indemnity agreements, agreements to defend others, and liquidated damages clauses, except that this exclusion shall not apply to a Claim where legal liability exists in the absence of such contract or agreement and arises from Your Wrongful Act or the Wrongful Act of Your subconsultants in the rendering of or failure to render Professional Services.

Indemnity clauses fall into three groupings. These are commonly called "broad form," "intermediate form," and "narrow form."

Broad Form Indemnity, as its name implies, requires the consultant to indemnify its client for all damages arising out of the project whether caused by the consultant, a third party, or even the client. An example of such a clause is:

> *Consultant shall indemnify, defend and save harmless the Client, and its officers, directors, employees and agents, from and against all liability, loss, cost or expense (including attorney's fees) by reason of liability imposed upon the Client, arising out of or related to Consultant's services, whether caused by or*

contributed to by the Client or any other party indemnified herein, unless caused by the sole negligence of the Client.

By the terms of this clause, you will indemnify your client for damages arising from your acts—regardless of whether those acts and omissions are negligent. By placing the word "negligence" after the other terms, it does not modify them but rather stands alone as a separate basis for indemnity.

Notice that this clause requires you to "defend" the owner against claims. This type of "defense" obligation is barred from coverage pursuant to the contractual liability exclusion of your policy. The language also requires that you indemnify the client for mere "allegations" without regard to whether or not there is negligence.

To trigger your indemnification obligation pursuant to this clause, there need only be a mere allegation that damages arose from your "professional services." Indemnification obligations not related to negligence are not covered by your policy.

Beware that the limited contractual liability coverage afforded by the typical professional liability policy is not intended by the carrier to respond to the kind of contractual obligations imposed upon you by the above-quoted contract language. You should seek to strike language requiring you to provide contractual liability coverage. If the client will not agree to strike it, then at a minimum the language should be amended to indicate that only limited contractual liability coverage is provided—meaning that your policy will contain an exclusion that provides a limited clarification of the contractual liability exclusion.

Intermediate Form Indemnity also shifts much risk to the consultant—but not as drastically as the broad form. It may state, for example, that the consultant will indemnify the client for all damages caused "in whole or in part" by the consultant. This language can be deceptively subtle. Many, if not most, courts interpret it to mean that if the consultant even slightly contributed to causing the damages, it will be required to indemnify the client for ALL of the damages, including those caused by the client's negligence.

An example of such a clause is as follows:

> *The Architect shall indemnify and hold harmless the Owner for all damages, losses, or claims that arise as a result, in whole or in part, from the negligence, or error, omissions, or failure to perform by the Architect, his employees, his agents, or his Consultants.*

This is an exceptionally bad clause. It is interpreted by courts to require the design professional to indemnify the owner for 100% of the damages incurred by the owner even if caused only in part (e.g., less than 1%) by the design professional. This is an unreasonable term and condition. It creates uninsurable risk for the design professional. Only the damages caused by the negligence of the design professional would be covered by the insurance.

Narrow Form Indemnity requires the consultant to indemnify its client only to the extent that damages are caused by the consultant's negligence. Of the three forms of indemnity, this is obviously the most reasonable. An example is as follows:

> *Consultant shall indemnify the client for damages arising out of the performance of professional services, but only to the extent caused by the negligent acts, errors or omissions of the Consultant.*

Keep in mind that consultants' professional liability policies are intended to respond only to damages caused by the negligence of the insured design professional. Exclusions in the policy generally bar coverage for contractual liability in which the consultant has assumed liability it would not have had under common law because it performed services negligently.

Beware of owner-generated clauses that initially may appear to provide negligence-based indemnity but in reality go further. Consider, for example, the following clause:

> Design Professional shall indemnify and hold harmless the Owner from any and all claims, damages, suits, and expenses caused by or arising out of the acts, omissions, errors or negligence of the Design Professional.

Because "negligence" is placed at the end of the phrase, it stands alone and does not modify the terms "acts," "errors," or "omissions." As a result, the design professional could be required to indemnify its client for damages arising out of even non-negligent errors and omissions. To remedy this situation, the clause could be amended to read: "…. arising out of the *negligent* acts, omissions or errors of the Design Professional." The key is to place the adjective "negligent" in front of the balance of the words.

A similar situation occurs in the following indemnity provision:

> Design Professional shall indemnify and hold harmless the Owner for all claims and damages arising out of the performance of professional services on this Project.

This clause could be appropriately revised by inserting the adjective "negligent" in front of "performance" so that the revised clause reads, "…. arising out of the *negligent* performance of professional services on this Project."

Conclusion: Carefully review the language of the contract's indemnity provision and remove any requirement that you "defend" your client in litigation. A requirement that you "defend" the client creates potentially uninsurable liability. In contrast to indemnification, which occurs after the fact and reimburses the client for its expenses, "defense" of the client requires you to expend money during the course of litigation before your liability has been determined.

Revise indemnity provisions to ensure that you indemnify the client *only to the extent* of damages caused by your negligence or the negligence of others for whom you are legally responsible. If the indemnity provision contains the language "in whole or in part," negotiate revised language stating that you are liable "only to the extent" of damages arising from your negligence.

The "contractual liability exclusion" in the professional liability policy states that there is no coverage for liability that you assume by contract that you would not have had at common law in the absence of the contract language. In other words, if you were negligent, your insurance covers you and the contractual liability is not an issue. If, however, you were not negligent, and the basis for the client's recovery against you is the contractual indemnification obligation, you have no coverage for that loss.

Pursuant to principles of common law, the design professional is legally responsible for its negligence, including a duty to indemnify its client for damages arising out of the design professional's negligence. A project owner, consequently, is adequately protected by common law even in the absence of any contract language specifically adding indemnification provisions. If you must have an indemnity clause, be sure it allocates risk to the parties in the best position to control and manage the risk. Consider the following:

> Consultant agrees to indemnify and hold harmless Client from and against any liabilities, damages, and costs arising out of the death or bodily injury to any person or the destruction or damage to any property, to the extent caused, during performance of services under this Agreement, by the negligent acts, errors and omissions of the Consultant or anyone for whom Consultant is legally responsible, subject to the limitations set forth in the Limitation of Liability article of this Agreement.

This clause is not intended for use without advice of counsel..

EJCDC E-500 (2002 Ed.) provides at Section 6.10.D for mutual indemnification for damages arising out of negligence, and specifically limits the indemnification to the percentage share of the indemnifying party's negligence.

> Percentage Share of Negligence. To the fullest extent permitted by law, a party's total liability to the other party and anyone claiming by, through, or under the other party for any cost, loss, or damages caused in part by the negligence of the party and in part by the negligence of the other party or any other negligent entity or individual, shall not exceed the percentage share that the party's negligence bears to the total

> negligence of Owner, Engineer, and all other negligent entities and individuals.

Clause may not be reproduced and used without permission of EJCDC.

A *mutual indemnification* provision creating mirror image obligations for the parties may seem more reasonable, and may result in more reasonable treatment by the project owner when negotiating the terms and conditions. Consider the following mutual indemnification provision from a manuscript contract:

> **Mutual Indemnification**
>
> Subject to the foregoing provisions, the Consultant agrees, to the fullest extent permitted by law, to indemnify and hold harmless the Client, its officers, directors, employees and agents from and against any liabilities, damages and costs (including reasonable attorneys fees and costs of defense) arising out of the death or bodily injury to any person or the destruction or damage to any property, to the extent caused, during the performance of Services under this Agreement, by the negligent acts, errors or omissions of the Consultant or anyone for whom the Consultant is legally responsible, subject to any limitations of liability contained in this Agreement. The Client agrees, to the fullest extent permitted by law, to indemnify and hold harmless the Consultant, its officers, directors, employees and agents from any liabilities, damages and costs (including reasonable attorneys fees and costs of defense) to the extent caused by the negligent acts, errors or omissions of the Client, the

> Client's contractors, consultants or anyone for whom Client is legally responsible.

This clause is not intended for use without advice of counsel.

Note this clause's good points:

- the indemnity is mutual;

- the indemnifying party only indemnifies for damages to the extent caused by its own negligence; and

- the indemnity obligation for the Consultant is capped at whatever limitations of liability have been negotiated into the contract in other clauses.

Educate your client to understand that your insurance will not cover you or provide any benefits to the client for costs you agree to incur that arise out of anything other than your negligence.

Inspection

Issue: Insurance Company risk management professionals routinely advise their insured design professionals to avoid using words in their contract that create a duty to "inspect" unless that is what is specifically called for by the scope of services. The design professional is not responsible for the contractor's work and cannot assure or guarantee that the contractor will meet all the details of the contract documents.

Unless a design professional is being retained specifically for the purpose of construction management services that entail inspection, the design professional will more typically agree only to "observe" or "review" the contractor's work for "general conformance" with the contract documents. It is not uncommon, however, to see contract language for general design services which transfer to the design professional significant responsibility and risk for inspection even though that is not within the scope of services for which the design professional is being paid.

One such Agreement, for example, included the following language:

> *The Architect shall visit the construction sites as often as is necessary to assure quality of the project ... to inspect the progress and quality of the Work and to determine if the Work is proceeding in accordance with Contract Documents ... and shall endeavor to guard the Owner against defects and deficiencies in the Work of the Contractor(s).*

Discussion: The term "inspection" is sometimes used in contracts generated by owners when "monitoring," "reviewing," or "observing" might be more appropriate. In describing the Architect's responsibilities as the project is reaching completion, the current AIA B141-1997 uses the term "inspection." Section 2.6.6.1 provides that, "The Architect shall conduct inspections to determine the date or dates of Substantial Completion...." But with respect to performing "Evaluations of the Work" as it progresses, Section 2.6.2.1. appropriately limits the Architect to visiting the site at appropriate intervals to become "generally" familiar with the progress and quality of the Work completed and to determine "in general" if the Work is being performed in a manner indicating that the Work, when fully completed, will be in accordance with the Contract Documents. The clause goes on to explain that the Architect is not responsible to make exhaustive or continuous on-site inspections.

When used to describe monitoring of the contractor's work, the term "inspections" may imply a greater responsibility than the Consultant intends to provide. The client may think that you are committing to police the project and through your "inspection" ascertain all instances where the contractor's personnel did not comply with the detailed plans and specifications and other contract documents. Some clients may even state in the contract that the purpose of the "inspection" is to assure the client that all problems are discovered and promptly reported to the client.

Another contract with inappropriate language for the scope of services stated:

> *Architect shall inspect the contractor's work, keep the Owner informed of the progress and quality of the Work, and shall protect Owner*

against defects and deficiencies in the Work of the contractors.

This should be revised to reflect that the Architect is not inspecting the contractor's work to guarantee that it has no defects. It can only "observe" the work and exercise reasonable care to determine that the work conforms generally with the contract documents. This is the industry standard and should be understood by an owner. After all, the Architect is not being compensated for the man-hours it would take to perform the function of watching everything done by the contractor to assure no defects or deficiencies. Moreover, the contractor must be held accountable for those defects and deficiencies rather than the Architect.

Conclusion: Unless you are specifically retained to perform "inspection" services, try to delete the words "inspect" or "inspection" in the contract and substitute them with "review," "monitor," and "observe."

Agreeing to observe whether the contractor's work is in "general conformance" with the design concept is realistic. This is a manageable risk, whereas "inspecting" whether the work meets the details of the plans and specifications creates much greater risk. AIA Document B-141-1997, Section 2.6.2.1, addresses the issue by explaining that the consultant will not be on site every day but will make site visits as appropriate to assess how the work is generally progressing. It states as follows:

> The Architect, as a representative of the Owner, shall visit the site at intervals appropriate to the stage of the Contractor's operations, or as otherwise agreed by the Owner and the Architect in Article 2.8, (1) to become generally familiar with and to keep the Owner informed about the progress and

quality of the portion of the Work completed, ... (3) to determine in general if the Work is being performed in a manner indicating that the Work, when fully completed, will be in accordance with the Contract Documents. However, the Architect shall not be required to make exhaustive or continuous on-site inspections to check the quality or quantity of the Work. The Architect shall neither have control over or charge of, nor be responsible for, the construction means, methods, techniques, sequences or procedures, or for safety precautions and programs in connection with the Work, since these are solely the Contractor's rights and responsibilities under the Contract Documents.

Clause may not be reproduced and used without permission of AIA.

A similar provision is contained in EJCDC E-500 (2002), Exhibit A, Section 1.05.A.7.a., as follows:

Make visits to the Site at intervals appropriate to the various stages of construction, as Engineer deems necessary, to observe as an experienced and qualified design professional the progress and quality of Contractor's executed Work. Such visits and observations by Engineer, and the Resident Project Representative, if any, are not intended to be exhaustive or to extend to every aspect of Contractor's Work in progress or to involve detailed inspections of Contractor's Work in progress beyond the responsibilities specifically assigned to Engineer in this Agreement and the Contract Documents, but rather are to be limited to spot checking, selective sampling, and similar methods of general observation of the Work based on Engineer's exercise of professional judgment as assisted by the Resident Project Representative, if any. Based on information obtained during such visits and observations, Engineer will determine in general if the Work is proceeding in accordance with the Contract Documents, and Engineer shall keep Owner informed of the progress of the Work.

Clause may not be reproduced and used without permission of EJCDC.

Insurance

Please review Chapter 9 for a more detailed discussion of design professional liability insurance, including what and who is covered by the policy, and how certain exclusions of the policy may impact your coverage for damages you may incur pursuant to the terms and conditions of your contracts with clients.

Issue 1: Limiting Contractual Obligations to What Can be Covered by an E&O Policy

Professional liability insurance is intended to cover you for your negligent acts, errors, and omissions. Breaches of warranty and contract are not covered—except to the extent the breaches result from negligent acts, errors, and omissions of the policy holder. Coverage for liability damages caused by anything other than your negligence is expressly excluded by the "contractual liability" exclusion.

Discussion: In one contract, the insurance provision stated that the design professional would obtain professional liability insurance "protecting from claims resulting from errors and omissions, or negligent acts arising out of the performance of professional services and operations under this Agreement."

The way the paragraph referenced above is written, it appears to expect insurance to cover all errors and omissions—regardless of whether they were negligent. The design professional should clarify to the owner that the professional liability policy, consistent with all such policies by all markets available today, limits coverage to damages caused by the design professional's negligence.

Impact of Indemnification Provisions on Coverage

Conclusion: When you see provisions requiring contractual liability, or "warranties" and "guarantees," you should immediately flag them as problem clauses. Some of these clauses are obvious. Others are subtle and harder to spot because they don't use language readily recognized as referring to "warranties" and "guarantees." If, for example, you agree to the "highest standard of care" instead of the "generally accepted standard," you may inadvertently warrant that your services will be the best, and will produce a perfect result. It may also be prudent to delete a reference in the indemnity clause that would require you to indemnify your client for breach of contract since this is not insurable absent negligence. In any event, your client has adequate legal recourse to sue for breach of contract without any need for a separate indemnity obligation.

Issue 2: Additional Insured Status

The professional liability carrier will rarely name an entity other than the design professional as an insured or additional insured under the professional liability section of the policy. Reasons for this include the fact that the owner of a project is not a licensed design professional and is not likely to commit a negligent design error for which it will need coverage under the professional liability policy. In addition, the owner is the party most likely to have damages for which it desires to sue the consultant and recover under the consultant's professional policy.

Discussion: A major problem with naming the client as an additional insured is that it creates potential remedies against the consultant that the owner would not otherwise have.

Conclusion: When your client requests to be named as an additional insured on the professional liability part of your insurance program, explain why the insurance carrier will not do this. Obtain a memorandum or letter from your insurance professional confirming this if necessary.

Issue 3: Obtaining Contractual Liability Coverage

If your contract with your client requires you to obtain contractual liability coverage, you may find yourself in breach of the contract if your insurance carrier will not agree to the broad form contractual liability coverage the client intended.

One owner-generated contract required the design professional to procure a professional liability policy with contractual liability coverage for the project owner. The contract provided:

> *The Engineer's contractual liability coverage must, at a minimum, protect the Owner to the extent of the following hold harmless agreement.*

Discussion: The language in the above-quoted Agreement went on to state that the Engineer will indemnify the owner for all expense *"caused in whole or in part by any negligent act or omission of the Engineer....."* Courts typically apply such language to mean that the Engineer is responsible for 100% of the damages as long as even only 1% was caused by the negligence of the Engineer. The design professional policy, however, will only pay for the damages to the extent caused by the negligence of the design professional or others for whom the design professional is legally responsible.

Contractual liability for anything other than damages caused by the design professional's negligence is excluded from coverage under the standard professional liability policy. Under these circumstances, the insurance company will not agree to provide contractual liability coverage for the liabilities the design professional agreed to in the contract.

Conclusion: The professional liability policy will only cover "contractual liability" to the extent that the design professional would have been liable for the damages in the absence of the contract language. This means that the policy only covers damages arising out of the design professional's negligence. You will need to negotiate out of the contract any requirement for contractual liability coverage that exceeds what is typically insured under a professional liability policy. If need be, obtain a letter/memorandum from your insurance broker and/or carrier to give to your client to help explain your position.

Limitation of Liability

Issue: An excellent way to limit the amount of liability undertaken by the design professional is the limitation of liability (LoL) clause. By including an LoL clause in your contract, you can better predict the extent of your potential liability and obtain appropriate coverage at a more reasonable cost.

Discussion: The rationale for capping liability for design professionals is that the small fee paid to the design firm does not justify the firm's assumption of all the risk. The project owner benefits from the sharing of risk because it is able to obtain innovative and cost-effective designs. The profit margin for design firms does not support their taking on unlimited risk for project owners. With today's high insurance premiums, one way to reduce the premiums to everyone's benefit is to include an LoL clause in more contracts. Underwriters generally consider the presence of an LoL clause when underwriting and pricing the risk.

Conclusion: Include a Limitation of Liability Clause in your own standard form contracts. Ask your client to include an LoL clause in its form contracts as well. Based on the success of many firms at getting these clauses into their contracts, and the further success in enforcing them in litigation, it is wrong to assume that you should not ask for and expect this clause. A typical clause may look like the following from EJCDC E-500 (2002), Exhibit I:

> 6.10.B *Limitation of Engineer's Liability*
>
> *Engineer's Liability Limited to Amount of Engineer's Compensation.* To the fullest extent

174 *Contract Guide for Design Professionals*

permitted by law, and notwithstanding any other provision of this Agreement, the total liability, in the aggregate, of Engineer and Engineer's officers, directors, partners, employees, agents, and Engineer's Consultants, and any of them, to Owner and anyone claiming by, through, or under Owner for any and all claims, losses, costs, or damages whatsoever arising out of, resulting from or in any way related to the Project or the Agreement from any cause or causes, including but not limited to the negligence, professional errors or omissions, strict liability or breach of contract, or warranty express or implied of Engineer or Engineer's officers, directors, partners, employees, agents, or Engineer's Consultants, or any of them, shall not exceed the total compensation received by Engineer under this Agreement.

This clause may not be reproduced without permission of EJCDC.

In this clause, various legal causes of action that are included in the limitation are specifically identified. There is a good reason for this. Some cases have held that if the LoL clause states that it applies to damages arising out of "negligence" and does not mention "breach of contract," an owner might sue for breach of contract and thereby avoid the limitation altogether. Note that the EJCDC provides several options for the client and engineer. You may offer specified "insurance" instead of a fixed dollar amount. Or you may offer a percentage of your fee.

Waiver of Consequential Damages. Even a client who does not want to include an LoL clause in the contract may be willing to include a mutual waiver of consequential damages. The AIA B141–1997, Section 1.3.6, provides:

Limitation of Liability **175**

> *Claims for Consequential Damages.* The Architect and the Owner waive consequential damages for claims, disputes or other matters in question arising out of or relating to this Agreement. This mutual waiver is applicable, without limitation, to all consequential damages due to either party's termination in accordance with Paragraph 1.3.8.

_{This clause may not be reproduced without permission of AIA.}

Note that if this clause is going to be agreed to in your contract with the owner, you should determine whether the owner is including a similar clause in its construction contract and, if so, request that the owner add language making the waiver of consequential damages by the contractor also applicable to claims against the design professional. You may otherwise be subject to Contractor Claims for equitable adjustment since the owner has the waiver from the contractor but you do not. As more states are discarding the "economic loss" rule and allowing contractors to sue design firms with whom they have no contract, it becomes increasingly important to include language in the construction contract to limit the contractor's remedies against the design professional.

Section 6.10.E of EJCDC Document E-500 (2002) provides a similar waiver, as follows:

> *Mutual Waiver.* To the fullest extent permitted by law, Owner and Engineer waive against each other, and the other's employees, officers, directors, agents, insurers, partners, and consultants, any and all claims for or entitlement to special, incidental,

> indirect, or consequential damages arising out of, resulting from, or in any way related to the Project.

This clause may not be reproduced without permission of EJCDC.

In negotiations concerning the waiver of consequential damages clause, one of the parties may ask for a definition of "consequential damages." As stated by one court, "There are two broad categories of damages *ex contractu*: direct (or general) damages and consequential (or special damages). Direct damages are those which arise 'naturally' or 'ordinarily' from a breach of contract; they are damages, which, in the ordinary course of human experience, can be expected to result from a breach.

Consequential damages are those which arise from the intervention of "special" circumstances" not ordinarily predictable. If damages are determined to be direct, they are compensable. If damages are determined to be consequential, they are compensable only if it is determined that the special circumstances were within the "contemplation" of both contracting parties.

Whether damages are direct or consequential is a question of law. Whether special circumstances were within the contemplation of the parties is a question of fact." (*Roanoke Hospital v. Doyle and Russell*, 215 Va. 796, 801 (1975).)

Although the AIA B141-1997 does not define "consequential damages," some of the elements of what AIA deems to be included within that term are set forth in AIA A201, Subparagraph 4.3.10 to include rental expenses, losses of use, income, profit, financing, business and reputation, and loss of management or employee productivity or the services of such persons.

Notice Requirements

Issue: Contractually specified time periods by which a design professional is to notify the owner of "occurrences," "events," "circumstances," or "changes" that may impact the schedule or cost of performance must be taken seriously. It is important that the prescribed time periods be realistic and that the Architect be aware of the time requirements and manage its services so as to meet them.

Discussion: When a contract states that the design professional must give notice of changes or requests for approval of additional services to specific, named individuals on behalf of the owner, the design professional must be aware of that requirement and provide notices to the appropriate individuals who have the exclusive authority to grant changes.

In a number of litigated cases, courts have held that project owners are excused from paying a design professional for "additional services" where the design professional failed to provide notice to the individual specified in the contract—despite the fact that notice had been given to others within the owner entity. A number of cases have also held that where the specified deadline for submitting notice, including information, data, and costing, has not been met, this may deprive the design professional of entitlement to payment for services.

In an apparent effort to expedite their projects and hold design professionals and contractors to strict schedules, some owners are arbitrarily establishing unrealistically short time periods in their contracts. Consider, for example, the following:

> Architect shall notify the Owner orally within forty-eight (48) hours after becoming aware of the occurrence of any event which will delay completion of the construction of the Project. Within five (5) days after providing oral notification, the Architect shall provide the Owner with a written confirmation, and such writing shall contain a detailed statement as to the event causing the delay, the exact length of the delay, and the steps the Owner should consider to minimize the impact of such event on the cost of construction and the time for completion of the Project.

A problem with establishing specific time periods for providing initial notice and then the follow-up detailed information is that each situation will be different. It is not possible to guarantee that the time periods can be met with the exercise of reasonable care. It may take the design professional longer than anticipated to analyze a unique and unanticipated situation. It may also take longer than anticipated to subsequently analyze the length of the delay and the efforts and costs by the contractor and design firm that may be needed to overcome the delay.

Conclusion: The design professional should review all notice and time requirements of the proposed contract and negotiate out those time periods that are mandatory and unreasonably short. Some flexibility for meeting time periods should be built into the contract language to recognize that meeting the professional standard of care may reasonably require that additional time be taken to analyze and report on the matters required.

Once time periods are agreed upon and included in the Agreement, be sure that all project and contract managers responsible for the project are aware of the notice requirements and adhere to them faithfully.

Owner Provided Data

Issue: Project owners should be contractually obligated to provide design firms with information and data in their possession. Design firms should be contractually permitted to rely upon site information and other information provided to them by the client. This includes reliance when preparing and pricing the initial proposal and also when performing services.

Discussion: Some project owners, however, are attempting to limit the design professional's reliance on such data. For example, consider this contract clause:

> *Consultant acknowledges that Owner provided documents, if any, including, without limitation, all plans, standards, specifications and drawings ("Owner's Documents") are submitted herewith by Owner to Consultant without any warranty whatsoever and are for conceptual and information purposes only. Consultant agrees and understands that it is Consultant's obligation and responsibility to properly engineer and design the subject matter of the Work Product. Consultant expressly assumes all Design and Products liability arising from or attributable directly or indirectly to Owner provided documents utilized by Consultant in the engineering and design of the subject matter of the Work Product....*

This puts all the risk on the consultant, including risk it is unable to manage and risk for which it would otherwise be entitled to an equitable adjustment for encountering.

Conclusion: Include a statement that the client intends for you to rely upon the information. An example clause from EJCDC E-500 (2002), Exhibit B, B2.01, is as follows:

> *In addition to other responsibilities of Owner as set forth in this Agreement, Owner shall at its expense:*
>
> A. Provide Engineer with all criteria and full information as to Owner's requirements for the Project, including design objectives and constraints, space, capacity and performance requirements, flexibility, and expandability, and any budgetary limitations; and furnish copies of all design and construction standards which Owner will require to be included in the Drawings and Specifications; and furnish copies of Owner's standard forms, conditions, and related documents for Engineer to include in the Bidding Documents, when applicable.

This clause may not be reproduced without permission of EJCDC.

Reliance upon information provided by the client is also set forth in EJCDC E-500, in the section entitled "Standards of Performance" at 6.01.D, which reads as follows:

> Subject to the standard of care set forth in Paragraph 6.01.A, Engineer and its Consultants may use or rely upon design elements and information ordinarily or customarily furnished by others, including, but not limited to, specialty contractors, manufacturers, suppliers, and the publishers of technical standards.

This clause may not be reproduced without permission of EJCDC.

AIA B141-1997 provides for the architect's reliance on information furnished by the owner. Section 1.2.3.7 provides as follows:

> The Architect shall be entitled to rely on the accuracy and completeness of services and information furnished by the Owner. The Architect shall provide prompt written notice to the Owner if the Architect becomes aware of any errors, omissions or inconsistencies in such services or information.

This clause may not be reproduced without permission of AIA.

Reliance upon client information also becomes important in addressing subsurface conditions and who has ultimate responsibility for them. Consider this clause from a manuscript contract addressing site information particularly as it affects responsibility for subsurface conditions:

> In the performance of the Services, the Consultant will take all reasonable precautions to avoid damage or injury to subsurface structures or utilities. Unless otherwise agreed in Attachment A, the Consultant will be responsible for contacting local authorities to obtain the location of public utilities and/or subterranean structures to the extent practicable. The Client agrees to provide the Consultant a complete set of site plans indicating utility locations and other underground structures, if available, and to hold the Consultant harmless and indemnify the Consultant for any claims, payments, or other liability, including costs and attorneys fees, incurred by the Consultant for any damages to subterranean

structures or utilities which are not correctly shown on such plans. If no plans are available or the location of such structures and utilities at the site cannot be determined, additional work, such as hand augering, may be required prior to subsurface work and will be billed to the Client in addition to the charges authorized in Attachment B hereto. The Client recognizes that subsurface conditions may vary from those encountered at the location where borings, surveys, tests, or explorations are made by the Consultant and that the data, interpretations, and recommendations of the Consultant are based solely upon the data available to the Consultant. The Consultant will be responsible for its own data, interpretation and recommendations, but shall not be responsible for the accuracy or validity of data provided by the Client or other sources, or for the interpretation by others of the information developed. While Consultant will take all reasonable precautions to minimize damage to the property, it is understood by the Client that in the normal course of work some reasonable damage may occur, the restoration of which is not part of this Agreement except to the extent agreed to in Attachment B.

This clause is not intended for use without advice of counsel.

An example from an environmental consulting contract is as follows:

Client's Responsibility

a) Client shall grant or cause to be granted to Consultant access to all sites as necessary for the performance of the Services under this Agreement.

b) Client shall furnish or cause to be furnished to Consultant all documents and information known to Client that relate to the identity, location, quantity, nature, or characteristics of any hazardous waste at or near the site. Consultant shall be entitled to rely on such information.

c) Unless otherwise required by law or set forth in this Agreement, Client shall be responsible for accurately locating, horizontally and vertically, and prominently marking any buried or concealed pipes, tanks, cables, utilities, or other manmade obstructions ("Underground Facilities") that may affect or be affected by Consultant's services. Consultant shall be entitled to rely on such information.

This clause is not intended for use without advice of counsel.

Ownership and Copyrights of Documents

Issue: Instruments of service produced by the design professional, including plans, specifications, drawings, opinions, reports, and calculations, have historically been treated as intellectual property belonging to the design firm that created it. This has been plainly stated in standard form contracts such as those published by the AIA, in Document B141, and EJCDC, in Document E-500.

Discussion: In contrast to the reasonableness of the AIA and EJCDC clauses, the provisions of the Construction Owners Association of America (COAA) Contract for Professional Services, (COAA Document P-300A, 2000 Ed.), Article 3.2, states the following:

> *The Construction Documents and any other documents or electronic media prepared by or on behalf of the Professional for the Project are the sole property of the Owner free of any retention rights of the Professional. The Professional hereby grants to the Owner an unconditional right to use, for any purpose whatsoever, the Construction Documents and any other documents or electronic media prepared by or on behalf of the Professional for the Project, free of any copyright claims, trade secrets or other proprietary rights with respect to such documents.*

Another COAA Contract example is as follows:

> *Owner shall own all right, title and interest in and to the Work Products [Instruments of Service], including all copyrights and proprietary rights therein. Consultant expressly acknowledges that the*

> *parties have agreed that all copyrightable aspects of the Work Products and all work in progress are to be considered "works made for hire" within the meaning of the Copyright Act of 1976, and that Owner is to be the "author" within the meaning of such Act. All such copyrightable works, as well as all copies of such works, shall be owned exclusively by Owner as its creation, and Consultant hereby expressly disclaims any interest in any of them. Consultant expressly acknowledges that Consultant is not a joint author and that the Work Products are not joint works under the Act.... Any ideas, conception, know-how or techniques to the Work Products shall be the sole and exclusive property of Owner.*

The above-quoted clauses give all rights to the owner. Ironically, this would prevent the design professional from using the details included in the Instruments of Service for any future projects. This would be so despite the fact that many of the general conditions, details, and even standard materials included in its Instruments of Service were items that the design professional had been using in its practice prior to its engagement with the client. It is possible that a court would interpret this contract language to give this client exclusive right to all such work despite the fact that it was previously used by the design professional.

Here are two more examples of language that give the Client too much ownership over the Instruments of Service and fail to provide adequate protection for the design professional whose documents are reused or misused:

> *The Architect hereby assigns to the Owner, without reservation, all copyrights to all project-related documents, models, computer drawings and other electronic expression, photographs, and other*

expression produced by the Architect. Among those documents are certain "Instruments of Service," including the design drawings and all drawings, specifications, and other documents that are included in the Contract Documents. The Owner's obligation to pay the Architect is expressly conditioned upon the Architect's obtaining a valid written assignment of copyrights from his Consultants in terms identical to those that obligate the Architect to the Owner as expressed in this subparagraph, which copyrights the Architect hereby assigns to the Owner. The Owner, in turn, hereby grants to the Architect a nonexclusive license to reproduce the documents for purposes relating directly to the Architect's performance of this Project and for the Architect's archival records. No other project-related documents may be reproduced for any other purpose without the express written permission of the Owner. No other copyrights are included in this grant of nonexclusive license to the Architect. This nonexclusive license shall terminate immediately upon the breach of this Agreement by the Architect.

An example of yet another bad clause is the following:

Ownership of Plans. – Client shall be the sole and exclusive owner of both the physical embodiment and any intangible rights in any and all plans, specifications, drawings, elevations, calculations, data ... and all other documents (in all cases whether preliminary or final) prepared by Consultant, or at Consultant's direction, or supplied by consultant or Client..... Client shall be free to utilize all such material and the contents thereof in any other development or project, provided that any such re-use shall not identify Consultant as the source of any such documents. Consultant may, at its election, retain one copy of such documents for reference purposes only.

Besides the fact that you are giving away your work for use on other projects without receiving any additional fee, the problem with allowing the owner to reuse your documents is that you lose control over how the documents are interpreted and used. This puts you at significant risk since you will not be able to make the revisions and changes to the documents that may be necessary before they can be used successfully on a new project. The liability exposure from such reuse should be carefully considered before you agree to permit it. Before agreeing to permit such reuse, it is advisable to negotiate specific disclaimers on the reuse and indemnification from the owner.

Conclusion: Architects should maintain the copyright of their documents and give the owner only a limited license to use them for a specific project. It is advisable to provide protection for the design professional by stating that the documents are the property of design professionals and are not to be reused without authorization. An example clause is as follows:

> Drawings, specifications and other documents, prepared by the Design Professional (DP) and the DP's consultants are Instruments of Service for use solely with respect to this Project. This includes documents in electronic form. The DP and the DP's consultants shall be deemed the authors and owners of their respective Instruments of Service and shall retain all common law, statutory and other reserved rights, including copyrights. The Instruments of Service shall not be used by the owner for future

> additions or alterations to this Project or for other projects, without the prior written agreement of the DP. Any unauthorized use of the Instruments of Service shall be at the Owner's sole risk and without liability to the DP and the DP's consultants.

This clause is not intended for use without advice of counsel.

When project owners create their own contract documents, it is critical that the design professional pay close attention to the language pertaining to ownership and use of the design documents. Clients are more frequently demanding that the documents be deemed their property to be reused at their will, without compensation, and without any liability protection afforded to the designer.

The problem with such clauses is that the designer loses the ability to control the use of its work product. Where a client uses some other firm to complete the design, the original architect is at greater risk because he is not on the project and is unable to correct the inevitable design errors that could be discovered and corrected as construction work progresses. By being on the project, the architect can interpret its drawings and specifications and cooperate with the contractor and owner to correct deficiencies or errors before they turn into problems.

Where the owner terminates the design professional and uses partially completed documents or takes the documents and modifies them for use on some other project, the risk is even greater. With this increased risk, it is prudent to require contract language with specific disclaimers and indemnification obligations on the part of the project owner.

Preserve and protect your interest in the Instruments of Service. You can do this while at the same time granting your client appropriate use of the documents for the limited purposes of the specific project. Section 6.03.E of EJCDC E-500 (2002) handles this by stating:

> Owner may make and retain copies of Documents for information and reference in connection with use on the Project by Owner. Engineer grants Owner a license to use the Documents on the Project, extensions of the Project, and other projects of Owner, subject to the following limitations: (1) Owner acknowledges that such Documents are not intended or represented to be suitable for use on the Project unless completed by Engineer, or for use or reuse by Owner or others on extensions of the Project or on any other project without written verification or adaptation by Engineer; (2) any such use or reuse, or any modification of the Documents, without written verification, completion, or adaptation by Engineer, as appropriate for the specific purpose intended, will be at Owner's sole risk and without liability or legal exposure to Engineer or to Engineer's Consultants; (3) Owner shall indemnify and hold harmless Engineer and Engineer's Consultants from all claims, damages, losses, and expenses, including attorneys' fees, arising out of or resulting from any use, reuse, or modification without written verification, completion, or adaptation by Engineer; (4) such limited license to Owner shall not create any rights in third parties.

This clause may not be reproduced without permission of EJCDC.

A clause like this one clearly sets forth the rights of the design professional. It also protects against the risk of liability that might otherwise arise out of reuse of the documents by an unauthorized person, including the project owner. The protection afforded by this clause is appropriate because if the documents are used on other projects without the design professional's knowledge and input, the designer will not be able to assess and revise the design for the new circumstances or new project. With such re-use, the design professional is not able to manage the risks that will naturally arise when design documents are used on a project.

If an owner is insistent that it be given ownership rights to the design documents, and you decide as a matter of business judgment that you are willing to grant such rights, you should seek to add an indemnity clause to protect you against claims that might arise out of the reuse of the documents. For example, you might include language like the following:

> The Owner agrees to hold harmless, indemnify, and defend the design professional against all damages, claims, and losses of any kind (including defense costs), arising out of any use of the plans and specifications on any other project, for additions to his project, or for completion of this project.

This clause is not intended for use without advice of counsel.

You should also be careful not to give away your own right to reuse the documents in the course of your future services for other clients. The EJCDC Document E-500, Section 6.03.A, handles this by stating:

> All Documents are instruments of service in respect to this Project, and Engineer shall retain an ownership and property interest therein (including the copyright and the right of reuse at the discretion of the Engineer) whether or not the Project is completed. . . .

This clause may not be reproduced without permission of EJCDC.

A clause in the AIA B141–1997, at Section 1.3.2.1, provides protection for the architect as follows:

> 1.3.2.1 Drawings, specifications and other documents, including those in electronic form, prepared by the Architect and the Architect's consultants are Instruments of Service for use solely with respect to this Project. The Architect and the Architect's consultants shall be deemed the authors and owners of their respective Instruments of Service and shall retain all common law, statutory and other reserved rights, including copyrights.
>
> 1.3.2.2 Upon execution of this Agreement, the Architect grants to the Owner a nonexclusive license to reproduce the Architect's Instruments of Service solely for purposes of constructing, using and maintaining the Project. . . .

This clause may not be reproduced without permission of AIA.

Permits

Issue: As a design professional, you are responsible for obtaining licenses and permits required for the performance of the services that will be performed under a professional services agreement with your client. This does not mean, however, that you should take on the responsibility for obtaining permits and governmental approvals that are typically obtained by project owners or their construction contractors.

Discussion: In one reported court decision, a design professional signed a contract containing a clause similar to the following:

> *Design Professional shall be responsible for obtaining all permits, licenses, and governmental approvals needed for the performance of this Project and the Design Professional's services.*

After the design firm completed preparing the design documents and the owner awarded construction to a construction contractor, a citizens' group filed suit to stop the project. A court granted a restraining order halting the project until an environmental impact study (EIS) was performed as required by the environmental laws of the state. It seems the project owner failed to obtain such a study prior to design and construction. It is also seems that conducting an EIS was not within the design professional's scope of service. Nevertheless, the court found the above-quoted clause so broad as to implicitly require that the design firm determine whether an EIS was required for the project and obtain a "negative declaration" from the state or any other environmental approvals necessary in order to construct the project. Delay attributed to the failure to obtain the required negative declaration and environmental approvals was, according to the court, the financial responsibility of the design professional in this case.

Conclusion: To avoid unintended consequences like these, be sure that the language of your contract does not require you to obtain licenses, permits, and approvals beyond those that are normal to your profession and your scope of services. Rather than agreeing to obtain permits, it may be wiser to agree only to *assist* the client in its own efforts to obtain permits. Consider the following clause:

> The Consultant will assist the Client in applying for those permits and approvals typically required by law for completion of the Project. All permit fees payable to an issuing authority shall be paid directly by the Client unless otherwise agreed in Attachment A.

This clause is not intended for use without advice of counsel.

Exhibit B, B2.01 of EJCDC E-500 (2002) provides that the project owner will have responsibility for permits and governmental approvals as follows:

> In addition to other responsibilities of Owner as set forth in this Agreement, Owner shall at its expense:
>
> . . .
>
> H. Provide reviews, approvals, and permits from all governmental authorities having jurisdiction to approve all phases of the Project designed or specified by Engineer and such reviews, approvals,

> and consents from others as may be necessary for completion of each phase of the Project.

<small>This clause may not be reproduced without permission of EJCDC.</small>

The risk of site access authorization or permits should typically be the responsibility of the project owner since it may be in the best position to deal with neighbors or adjacent landowners.

Beware of contract language requiring the design professional to obtain such authorization or permits from third party landowners who may in turn require unobtainable insurance requirements or onerous indemnity agreements that they probably would not do if they were dealing directly with the project owner and being paid by the owner for access.

Reliance on Information Provided by Others

Issue: The design professional should be able to rely upon site information and other information provided to it by the client when preparing and pricing its proposal, and when performing its services. Some project owners, however, are attempting to limit the design professional's reliance on such data. Consider this contract clause:

> *Consultant acknowledges that Owner provided documents, if any, including, without limitation, all plans, standards, specifications and drawings ("Owner's Documents") are submitted herewith by Owner to Consultant without any warranty whatsoever and are for conceptual and information purposes only. Consultant agrees and understands that it is Consultant's obligation and responsibility to properly engineer and design the subject matter of the Work Product. Consultant expressly assumes all Design and Products liability arising from or attributable directly or indirectly to Owner provided documents utilized by Consultant in the engineering and design of the subject matter of the Work Product...*

This puts all the risk on the design professional, including risks that it is unable to manage and for which it would otherwise be entitled to an equitable adjustment.

An article in another contract provided:

> *Owner shall endeavor to make available to the Architect such information as is requested by the Architect and in the Owner's possession regarding the Project and existing conditions at the Project*

200 *Contract Guide for Design Professionals*

> site. The Owner may also provide Architect with certain assumptions concerning the Project. The Architect shall evaluate and verify the accuracy of all such information and assumptions.... The Architect shall not rely solely on existing information, such as utility or record drawings. Field and other investigations shall be thorough and detailed to permit an accurate understanding of existing conditions. The Architect shall also investigate, observe and analyze concealed conditions at the Project site to determine that the Construction Documents reflect accurately the existing conditions at the Project site....

Discussion: The above clauses severely limit the design professional's ability to rely upon the information and data concerning the site provided by the owner. Moreover, an affirmative duty has been created requiring the design professional to conduct its own detailed site investigations—even of concealed conditions. This is unreasonable and unrealistic, and creates unmanageable risks for the design professional. Owners generally do not expect design professionals to spend the time, money, and resources conducting the type of investigations and studies suggested by the above-quoted clauses, and owners certainly don't expect to pay for such services.

Conclusion: Include a statement that the client intends for you to rely upon the information. An example clause is 1.2.3.7 of AIA B141–1997, which provides:

> The Architect shall be entitled to rely on the accuracy and completeness of services and information furnished by the Owner. The Architect shall provide prompt written notice to the Owner if

Reliance on Information Provided by Others 201

> the Architect becomes aware of any errors, omissions or inconsistencies in such services or information.

This clause may not be reproduced without permission of AIA.

Reliance upon information provided by the client is also set forth in Section 6.01.D of EJCDC E-500 (2002) which provides:

> Subject to the standard of care set forth in Paragraph 6.01.A, Engineer and its Consultants may use or rely upon design elements and information ordinarily or customarily furnished by others, including, but not limited to, specialty contractors, manufacturers, suppliers, and the publishers of technical standards.

This clause may not be reproduced without permission of EJCDC.

EJCDC Document E-500, Exhibit B at B2.01 sets forth specific responsibilities of the project owner, as follows:

> In addition to other responsibilities of Owner as set forth in this Agreement, Owner shall at its expense:
>
> A. Provide Engineer with all criteria and full information as to Owner's requirements for the Project, including design objectives and constraints, space, capacity and performance requirements, flexibility, and expandability, and any budgetary limitations; and furnish copies of all design and construction standards which Owner will require to

be included in the Drawings and Specifications; and furnish copies of Owner's standard forms, conditions, and related documents for Engineer to include in the Bidding Documents, when applicable.

This clause may not be reproduced without permission of EJCDC.

Responsibility for the Services of Others

Issue: A design firm is legally responsible to its client for the acts, errors, and omissions of its subconsultants. Design firms are not responsible for the acts and omissions of contractors and other design professionals that are under contract directly with the project owner. It is not uncommon, however, for project owners to begin a project by contracting with more than one consultant and to later decide it prefers to have only one prime consultant, with all the others working under subcontract to that prime.

In a number of reported court decisions, the lead design professional on a project accepted assignment by the owner of contracts with other consultants with whom the owner had previously contracted for provision of specialized services such as geotechnical, environmental, facility planning, and others. When this happens, the lead design professional becomes contractually liable for the actions of firms that it did not select and over which it had no control.

Discussion: Some owner-generated contracts give the project owner unfettered discretion to assign its contracts to a single design firm. One contract provided as follows:

> *Owner may assign to Architect, and Architect agrees to accept the assignment of certain design professional contracts entered into by Owner prior to the execution of this Agreement. Pursuant to Article 11, Architect agrees to be responsible for the errors, omissions and negligent acts of such design professionals as though they had been retained by Architect initially.*

Owners have made some significant claims against design firms based on errors in the services provided by the owner's design professional that had been assigned to the Architect. If you sign a contract containing language like that quoted above, you are taking on contractual responsibility for risks that you would not have been responsible for at common law, and this may subject you to liability that is excluded from coverage under your professional liability policy.

Conclusion: Don't accept assignment of others' contracts without doing serious due diligence and obtaining appropriate assignment of risks. Get the advice of your legal counsel and insurance advisor before agreeing to the assignment of subcontracts. They may be able to provide language you can negotiate into the contract with the owner to state that the Prime Architect accepts an assignment of contracts but with no responsibility for acts, errors, and omissions of those firms that were committed prior to the assignment of the contract. It may also be advisable to draft contract language to limit your liability arising out of the services performed by these other firms.

Schedule
(Timeliness of Performance)

When delays occur in the performance of your services for reasons other than your negligence, you should not be held responsible for those delays. There should be a way for you to be excused for not completing the services by the scheduled completion date if the delay is caused by others. In some cases, you should be paid additional compensation for the delay, especially when that delay is caused by the owner or the construction contractor over whom you have no responsibility. Some clients, however, seek to make the consultant responsible for all delays and assess costs against the consultant for all delays.

Issue 1: Time of the Essence Clauses

Consultants are sometimes required to perform services under a contract stating "time is of the essence." Such a clause may have the unintended effect of putting timeliness ahead of the cautious exercise of due professional care.

Discussion: Consider this clause:

> *Consultant agrees that no charges or claim for damages shall be made by it for any delays or hindrances from any cause whatsoever during the progress of any portion of the services specified in the Agreement. Such delays or hindrances, if any, shall be compensated for by an extension of time for such reasonable period as the Owner may decide...*

This is a classic "no damage for delay" clause for a construction contract. It is rare for a design services contract, yet it is appearing in more of them. Another bad clause is the following:

> *Time is of the essence in performance of the Services described in this Agreement. Unless extended by mutual written agreement of the Parties, Consultant's obligation to perform the Services to be provided under the terms of this Agreement shall commence on the Effective Date and be completed on or before the scheduled termination date.*

This clause fails to allow for unforeseen circumstances or for situations where the exercise of an appropriate standard of care may require additional time for performance.

Conclusion: One way to address the owner's need for completion to be accomplished by a specified date while at the same time giving some reasonable time extension to the design professional when necessary, is to include a clause stating that the Consultant will exercise diligence to complete its services on the schedule established for the project, as may be consistent with the standard of care required for the services. An example is as follows:

> Consultant agrees to exercise diligence in the performance of its services consistent with the agreed upon project schedule, subject, however, to the exercise of the generally accepted standard of care for performance of such services.

This clause is not intended for use without advice of counsel.

The AIA B141–1997 addresses this issue at Clause 1.2.3.2, by providing the following:

> The Architect's services shall be performed as expeditiously as is consistent with professional skill and care and the orderly progress of the Project....

This clause may not be reproduced without permission of AIA.

In practical terms, this means that the design professional is committed to performing its services on the agreed upon schedule as far as can consistently be done within the generally accepted standard of care for performance of such services. Under the terms of this clause, if you fail to meet the schedule you will not automatically be liable to your client for damages on a warranty type basis. If the untimely performance results from owner interference or changes, for example, rather than from your negligence, that untimeliness may be an excusable delay if you have included appropriate contract language.

Issue 2: Responsibility for Contractor's Schedule

Some contracts attempt to shift responsibility to the design professional for assuring that the contractor performs its work on schedule. Consider the following clause:

> In the event the Construction Contractor fails to substantially complete the Project on or before the substantial completion date specified in its agreement with Owner, and the failure to substantially complete is caused in whole or in part by a negligent act, error or omission of the Design Professional, then Design Professional shall pay to

> *Owner its proportional share of any claim or damages to Contractor arising out of the delay.*

The clause goes on to establish liquidated damages for delays in construction that go beyond milestones for different phases of the work. As a result, the Design Professional may be required to pay the liquidated damages that the contractor would otherwise have to pay, in the event that the delay is attributed to the Design Professional's negligence.

Discussion: In another contract, a clause went even further with its assignment of responsibility for the project schedule to the Architect. It provided:

> *In addition to preparing the Project Schedule, Architect shall assist the Contractor to prepare a Critical Path Method ("CPM") or other approved Project construction schedule for the construction Project which shall integrate the Architect's services with the Contractor's Work and with the Owner's occupancy requirements for the Project.*

It would appear from this clause that the Architect is assuming responsibility for creating the project schedule and the CPM schedule that the contractor will use. This gives the Architect too much scheduling responsibility and may so insinuate the Architect into the contractor's scheduling responsibility that it will give the contractor a legal excuse for missing deadlines. This may entitle the contractor to additional time and cost for eventual changes to the schedule for which the contractor alone should have been responsible.

Conclusion: At a minimum, the clause should be revised to state that the contractor is solely responsible for his schedule, including his means, methods, and procedures for obtaining that schedule.

Issue 3: Time Limitations on Design Professional Response to Contractor RFI

Some contracts establish specific time frames for the design professional to review contractor requests for information (RFIs), shop drawings, and change order requests. One contract, for example, reads:

> *Architect shall respond to Contractor's request for information within 48 hours after receipt of a request or such earlier time as is necessary to maintain the Construction Schedule.*

Discussion: This short time frame may create an impossibility. Despite diligent efforts by the design professional, it may be impossible to analyze the situation and respond within such a short time frame. This could turn into a situation where the contractor knows of its need for information but procrastinates on its request to the point of creating a critical path delay—possibly to establish its own right to time and/or cost increase.

Conclusion: At a minimum, when a time frame is specified, an exception should be added to the time requirement to permit "additional time as necessary for the Architect to review the matter and act in a manner consistent with the Standard of Care." Delete language such as "time is of the essence." Agree only to complete your services in a timely manner consistent with the exercise of due care. If the client insists on subjecting you to a "time is of the essence" clause, and holding you to a strict time deadline, consider including a clause for "Suspension," "Timeliness of

Performance," or "Force Majeure" that will excuse untimely performance that was caused by delays beyond your control.

An example from EJCDC E-500 (2002), Section 3.02, provides in pertinent part:

> A. Engineer shall complete its obligations within a reasonable time. Specific periods of time for rendering services are set forth or specific dates by which services are to be completed are provided in Exhibit A, and are hereby agreed to be reasonable. ****
>
> E. If Engineer fails, through its own fault, to complete the performance required in this Agreement within the time set forth, as duly adjusted, then Owner shall be entitled to the recovery of direct damages resulting from such failure.

This clause may not be reproduced without permission of EJCDC.

As stated in the issue portion of this topic, the design professional should seek to add some additional time and flexibility to its turn-around time for responding to RFIs and other requests by contractors.

Scope of Service

Issue: Lack of clarity in the contract concerning the scope of service, including what is to be performed as basic service and what are additional services, is one of the greatest causes of disputes between owners and their design professionals. This is an area of risk that can be effectively managed by carefully defining the scope of the services to be performed so that there is no misunderstanding nor any unmet expectations by the parties.

Discussion & Conclusion: Basic Services should be specified in reasonable detail in the contract or as an attachment to the contract. Services that might reasonably be provided for the project but which are excluded from your Basic Services may be listed as "Additional Services" that are to be paid for as requested by the owner. See, for example, AIA B141-1997, Article 2.8. *Schedule of Services.*

Section 2.8.1 provides for payment as a change in services to the architect for design and contract administration services beyond specified limits.

Section 2.8.2 provides for payment as a change in services to the architect for eight specific categories of services. These include reviewing contractor submittals, responding to excessive RFIs, responding to change orders, evaluating an extensive number of contractor claims, evaluating contractor's equipment substitution proposals, and several other matters.

Section 2.8.3 provides that the architect will perform a list of 22 specified services only if designated in writing by the client as part of the contract. This three-part article communicates the intent of the parties and helps prevent ambiguity and disagreement concerning what services are to be performed and whether they are to be performed as part of basic or additional services.

It may even be prudent to list services that will be specifically excluded when you know those services may be needed for the project but the owner has chosen to have them performed by others. Environmental service is a good example of something that is necessary for a particular project but which may be excluded from your scope of service.

To avoid an owner later claiming the design professional should have detected and corrected environmental issues, you may include a clause specifically stating that you are not responsible for environmental services. This can be done in the AIA B141 document at Section 2.8.3 by filling in the boxes that identify "Responsibility" for the 22 items listed.

For each item that is not to be performed by the Architect, the form provides space to write that it is either "Owner" responsibility or "Not Provided." This latter category can be used to show that the service, such as "Environmental Studies and Reports," is not being provided by either the architect or the owner.

Severability & Survival

Issue: If a court finds that a contract provision is contrary to law or public policy, it may find the clause to be unenforceable and apply any applicable statutory or common law to that issue instead. It is even possible in some situations that a court might determine that the entire contract is void because of one clause.

Discussion: Instead of taking the chance that the contract will be voided or changed to provide something other than the original intent of the parties, it is prudent to protect against this by including corrective language in the contract.

Conclusion: Include a clause in the contract stating that in the event that one or more terms of the contract are determined to be invalid or unenforceable, the balance of the contract will nevertheless remain in full force and effect. This is a "severability" clause. Another clause that may be used in conjunction with this is a "survival" clause. It provides that in the event a clause is deemed invalid or unenforceable, it will be revised to be consistent with the law but still reflect the intent of the parties to the greatest extent permitted by law. These two concepts are often merged into a single clause.

An example of a severability clause stating that the invalidity of a clause will not impact the validity of the balance of the contract, and that the offending clause will be reformed to make it enforceable, is the following:

> The various provisions herein shall be deemed to be separate and severable, and the invalidity of any of them shall in no manner affect or impair the validity

or enforcement of the remaining provisions. Any provision held to be void or unenforceable shall be reformed to replace the provision with a valid and enforceable provision which expresses the original intention of the parties as closely as possible.

This clause is not intended for use without advice of counsel.

Consider using a clause like EJCDC E-500 (2002), Section 6.11.C:

Severability. Any provision or part of the Agreement held to be void or unenforceable under any Laws or Regulations shall be deemed stricken, and all remaining provisions shall continue to be valid and binding upon Owner and Engineer, who agree that the Agreement shall be reformed to replace such stricken provision or part thereof with a valid and enforceable provision that comes as close as possible to expressing the intention of the stricken provision.

This clause may not be reproduced without permission of EJCDC.

Some contract clauses are so important that you will want them to survive the completion or termination of the contract. These might include, for example, indemnification and limitations of liabilities clauses. Section 6.11.B of EJCDC E-500 (2002) provides for survival of certain terms and conditions with the following language:

Survival. All express representations, waivers, indemnifications, and limitations of liability included in this Agreement will survive its completion or termination for any reason.

<small>This clause may not be reproduced without permission of EJCDC.</small>

Notice that the clause below, in addition to addressing severability of the clause, also includes language dealing with waiver by either party of enforcement of a clause. Some contracts add a separate paragraph to address waiver of conditions, but as seen here, it can also be included in this clause.

If any one or more of the provisions contained in this Agreement, for any reason, are held to be invalid, illegal, or unenforceable in any respect, such invalidity, illegality or unenforceability shall not affect any other provisions hereof and this Agreement shall be construed as if such invalid, illegal, or unenforceable provision had never been contained herein. One or more waivers by either party of any provision, term, condition, or covenant shall not be considered a waiver of any provision, term, condition, or covenant or the subsequent breach of the same by the other party.

<small>This clause is not intended for use without advice of counsel.</small>

Note that the titles to the articles do not necessarily completely describe the content that will follow. Don't assume you know the provisions of a clause just because you've read other clauses with the same title in other contracts. Always read the language to be sure it does what you have been accustomed to seeing it do from past experience.

Shop Drawings

Issue: Through the shop drawing review process, clients sometimes expect more of a design professional than is reasonable or even within the design professional's scope of service stated elsewhere in the contract. For example, consider this clause:

> *The Design Professional is responsible for keeping the Owner completely apprised of the Project during the Construction Phase.... and shall be responsible for examining and approving shop drawings and correcting shop drawings.*

Discussion: By "approving" shop drawings, it might be argued by the contractor or the owner that the design professional has considered the details of the drawings and agreed that the contractors' details, measurements, and methods are accurate and satisfactory.

Design professionals have been advised in a number of training courses to avoid using words like "approval" of shop drawings. It is noted, however, that the AIA B141—1997 now utilizes language whereby the Architect "approves" shop drawings. But under the AIA documents, contractors remain responsible for "correcting shop drawings" after rejection by the design professional. The design professional does not correct the contractor's shop drawings.

By "assuring" contractor compliance with the plans and specifications or by taking on responsibility to "correct" shop drawings, the design professional may unintentionally accept legal responsibility for risks and responsibilities that more appropriately belong to the construction contractor. If possible, some clarifying language in the contract is useful to establish that regardless of what language is used to describe what the design professional does during its review of shop drawings, it remains the exclusive responsibility of the contractor to satisfy the details of the design.

Conclusion: Include language in the contract to limit your role in reviewing shop drawings. Paragraph A1.05.A.11 of the EJCDC E-500 (2002 Ed.) provides reasonable language, as does the AIA B141—1997, Paragraph 2.6.4.1, which provides:

> The Architect shall review and approve or take other appropriate action upon the Contractor's submittals such as Shop Drawings, Product Data and Samples, but only for the limited purpose of checking for conformance with information given and the design concept expressed in the Contract Documents. . . . Review of such submittals is not conducted for the purpose of determining the accuracy and completeness of other details such as dimensions and quantities, or for substantiating instructions for installation or performance of equipment or systems, all of which remain the responsibility of the Contractor as required by the Contract Documents.

This clause may not be reproduced without permission of AIA.

In addition to getting reasonable language in the contract, you should also take care that your shop drawing stamp contains language that manages your risk. Include disclaimers that clearly define what is meant by the review and that expressly state that the contractor remains fully responsible for meeting all requirements of the contract and using its own means, methods, and procedures and remains responsible for assuring the accuracy of all measurements, etc. It is important that your stamp makes it clear that you are reviewing only whether the information in the drawings conforms generally with the design.

EJCDC E-500, Exhibit A, at A.1.05.A.11 provides:

> *Shop Drawings and Samples.* Review and approve or take other appropriate action in respect to Shop Drawings and Samples and other data which Contractor is required to submit, but only for conformance with the information given in the Contract Documents and compatibility with the design concept of the completed Project as a functioning whole as indicated by the Contract Documents. Such reviews and approvals or other action will not extend to means, methods, techniques, sequences, or procedures of construction or to safety precautions and programs incident thereto. Engineer shall meet any Contractor's submittal schedule that Engineer has accepted.

This clause may not be reproduced without permission of EJCDC.

EJCDC also provides for the situation where the design firm's role is limited to design phase services and the designer will have no role during the construction phase. In order to advise the owner of the risks inherent in proceeding in this manner, and to limit the designer's liability that may arise out of the use of its documents during construction, it includes the following clause:

6.02   Design Without Construction Phase Services

A. If Engineer's Basic Services under this Agreement do not include Project observation, or review of the Contractor's performance, or any other Construction Phase services, then (1) Engineer's services under this Agreement shall be deemed complete no later than the end of the Bidding or Negotiating Phase; (2) Engineer shall have no design or shop drawing review obligations during construction; (3) Owner assumes all responsibility for the application and interpretation of the Contract Documents, contract administration, construction observation and review, and all other necessary Construction Phase engineering and professional services; and (4) Owner waives any claims against the Engineer that may be connected in any way thereto.

This clause may not be reproduced without permission of EJCDC.

Site Safety

Issue: Site safety is generally the responsibility of the contractors on the project. The contractor is best able to perform this function because it has direct responsibility for the work at the site. The contractor's injured workers sometimes seek to recover damages (in excess of what is available from their employer's worker's compensation) from the design professional. They may argue that by virtue of the design professional's contract language or its actions in the field, the design professional controlled the work site and is, therefore, liable for the construction worker's injuries. Workers sometimes argue that the consultant knew of a danger and failed to do anything to prevent the plaintiff from sustaining injury.

Injured workers may also argue that the consultant knew of dangerous conditions and took various actions to correct the problem—such as communicating directives to the general contractor—and that this demonstrates the consultant had the authority to control or actually did control the work at the jobsite.

The case law in this area has become confusing and varies from state to state. In addition to suits by workers, the U.S. Department of Labor has also weighed in by bringing actions against consultants arguing that they are liable for worker injuries under the OSHA requirements.

Discussion:

The extent to which design professionals have responsibility and liability for job site safety continues to be debated in courts around the country, with widely divergent results. This makes it difficult to provide uniform advice or counsel to design professionals. Risk management consultants and attorneys are generally quick to advise design professionals to obtain legal advice specific to the law of their individual state, rather than rely upon general educational information that may be provided in risk management workshops and nationally distributed books such as this one.

You should obtain the advice of local counsel and not rely upon the general principles presented herein. Having provided that caveat and disclaimer, this safety discussion will provide an overview of recent case decisions, as well as some generic risk management ideas for design professionals concerned about their potential responsibility for the safety of individuals other than their own employees.

Site safety is primarily the responsibility of the construction contractor. Prosecuting the work to meet the specifications and maintain a safe job site is within the contractor's means, methods, and procedures of performing the work. Construction contracts such as standard AIA contract forms expressly state that the contractor has responsibility for site safety. The design professional contract form typically states that the design professional is not responsible for site safety, and that the construction contractor has sole responsibility for it.

In such circumstances, a contractor that is told by the design professional to perform its work in a manner different than the contractor intended may have a basis for alleging entitlement to a change order for extra costs incurred in making the change, plus any delay and impact costs that might be caused by the change. In addition, where the design professional has involved itself in site safety decisions and exercised control over the work or workers' safety, some courts have looked beyond the written language of the contract and held the design professional to be responsible for site safety based on its actions in the field that created implied authority to control the work despite the contract language to the contrary.

Several court decisions have held that once a design professional has insinuated itself into site safety responsibility by actions such as instructing laborers to get out of unshored trenches, the design professional has a continuing obligation to stay involved in site safety. It cannot subsequently ignore safety problems and assert that they are the exclusive responsibility of the contractor. In other words, if a design professional saved the life of a worker by ordering him out of an unsafe trench, and a few days later that individual died in the trench that was still unsafe, courts have held the design professional responsible.

Partly as a reaction to such decisions, some (or perhaps many) design professionals have adopted a position that they will not see or report safety problems that they observe. The idea is that if you don't say anything to anyone about safety, you can't inadvertently create legal responsibility that goes beyond your contract requirements.

In the case of *Carvalho v. Toll Brothers and Developers*, 675 A.2d 209 (N.J. 1996), however, the court held that when an engineer observes work and inferably has actual knowledge of a dangerous condition, the engineer has a duty to exercise reasonable care to the worker. Although the contract did not give the engineer responsibility for site safety, the court stated that, "the engineer's responsibilities for ensuring compliance with the plans and the rate of work progress, including the proper handling of utilities that crossed the trench, implicated safety concerns."

The court in *Carvalho* further stated that the engineer had authority to halt work that was not in compliance with the specifications, and that this gave the engineer "sufficient control to halt work until adequate safety measures were taken." What this decision appears to mean for engineers in New Jersey is that if they have actual knowledge of dangerous job site conditions that could foreseeably cause harm to workers, they have a duty to exercise reasonable care to avert harm to the workers, regardless of what their contract might say to the contrary.

In contrast, a Pennsylvania court in the case of *Herczeg v. Hampton Township Municipal Authority and Bankson Engineers*, 766 A.2d 866 (2001), recently declined to impose liability on an engineer in similar circumstances. A construction worker (Steven Wagner) died while working in an unshored trench. The complaint alleged that the engineer ("Bankson") was the project representative for the owner, and had actual knowledge that Wagner was working in a dangerously unsafe trench "in that the trench had no shoring or bracing in violation of Bankson's own specifications, federal law and industry practices."

It was further claimed that the risk of serious injury or death was reasonably foreseeable and that Bankson's representative took no steps to warn the workers or to correct the situation. Under those alleged conditions, the plaintiff asserted that the engineer breached a duty owed to the decedent and was liable for his resultant death.

In its answer to the complaint, the engineer asserted that it had no knowledge of an unsafe condition and no duty regarding the allegations. It also alleged that it had no authority to control the contractor's work and never assumed by contract or conduct any responsibility for job site safety.

The trial court granted the engineer's motion to dismiss the complaint for failure to state a cause of action. On appeal, the appellate court affirmed the dismissal, stating, "The courts in this Commonwealth have consistently refused to impose a duty on design professionals to protect workers from hazards on a construction site unless there was an undertaking, either by contract or course of conduct to supervise or control the construction and/or maintain safe conditions on the site."

In this particular case, the court further explained the plaintiff's theory of liability as follows: "Appellant argues the traditional principles of negligence law should impose a duty on an engineer to exercise reasonable care for the safety of the general contractor's workers when the engineer has actual knowledge of dangerous working conditions that create foreseeable risk of serious injury to those workers. She submits this is true even where the contract places the responsibility for safety on the general contractor and the engineer's plans and specifications did not create the dangerous conditions. We cannot agree."

With regard to the applicability of *Carvalho*, the Pennsylvania court stated, "We are not persuaded that the rationale expressed in these cases warrants the establishment of a new rule of law fastening liability based strictly upon an assertion of actual knowledge of unsafe work site conditions." The court further stated, "We reject any notion that a duty arises based solely upon an engineer's actual knowledge of dangerous conditions.... If someone is under no legal duty to act, it matters not whether that person is actually aware of a dangerous condition.... Conversely, if someone by contract or course of conduct has undertaken the responsibility for worker safety that person may still be liable even in the absence of actual knowledge of the dangerous condition if they should have known of the condition."

This decision by the Pennsylvania court provides a well-reasoned discussion of the different legal theories that may apply, depending upon the jurisdiction where the project is located.

Practical Ideas: Expressly state in the contract any limitations upon your responsibilities with regard to jobsite safety. Include a provision stating that the general contractor is responsible for overall site safety, including the safety of its own employees.

Affirmatively state in the contract that you are not responsible for the safety program and procedures of the general contractor or of the project site. State also that *to the extent you observe and review contractor's work* it is only for the purpose of confirming the contractor's general conformance with the contract documents and not for the purpose of reviewing its safety procedures.

Require your client to include a provision in its construction contract requiring the contractor to indemnify you for any claim arising out of injuries or death of an employee of the contractor. Consider the following example:

> The Consultant will be responsible only for its activity and that of its employees and subconsultants at the job site. Neither the professional activities of the Consultant, nor the presence of the consultant or its employees and sub-consultants at a work site, shall relieve the Client or its contractor(s) of their obligations, duties and responsibilities including, but not limited to, construction means, methods, sequence, techniques or procedures necessary for performing, superintending and coordinating the Work in accordance with the contract documents and any health or safety precautions required by any

regulatory agencies. The Consultant and its personnel have no authority to exercise any control over any construction contractor or its employees in connection with their work or any health or safety programs or procedures; however, the Consultant reserves the right to report to the Client any unsafe condition observed at the site without altering the foregoing. The Client agrees that the General Contractor shall be solely responsible for job site safety, and warrants that this intent shall be carried out in the Client's contracts with the General Contractor by which the Consultant and sub-consultants shall be indemnified by the General Contractor and shall be made additional insureds under the General Contractor's policies of general liability insurance.

This clause is not intended for use without advice of counsel.

Another example is as follows:

The Consultant will be responsible only for its activity and that of its employees and subcontractors at the job site. Neither the professional activities of the Consultant, nor the presence of the Consultant or its employees or sub-consultants at a work site, shall relieve the Client or its contractor(s) of their obligations, duties and responsibilities including, but not limited to, construction means, methods, sequence techniques or procedures necessary for performing, superintending and coordinating the contractor's work in accordance with its applicable contract documents and any health and safety requirements of the Client and regulatory agencies.

> The Consultant and its personnel have no authority to exercise any control over the Client, its contractors(s) or their employees or subcontractors in connection with their work or any health and safety programs or procedures; however, the Consultant reserves the right to report to the Client any unsafe condition observed at the site without altering the foregoing.

_{This clause is not intended for use without advice of counsel.}

> Beware that despite the contract language, the courts in some states may impose liability upon the design professional that has actual knowledge of dangerous conditions and does nothing to prevent injury to workers.

EJCDC E-500 (2002), Section 6.01, provides:

> I. Engineer shall not at any time supervise, direct, or have control over Contractor's work, nor shall Engineer have authority over or responsibility for the means, methods, techniques, sequences, or procedures of construction selected or used by Contractor, for security or safety at the Site, for safety precautions and programs incident to the Contractor's work in progress, nor for any failure of Contractor to comply with Laws and Regulations applicable to Contractor's furnishing and performing the Work.

_{This clause may not be reproduced without permission of EJCDC.}

Further, Exhibit D, D1.01.B, in describing additional services that the design profession may perform, states:

> Through such additional observations of Contractor's work in progress and field checks of materials and equipment by the RPR and assistants, Engineer shall endeavor to provide further protection for Owner against defects and deficiencies in the Work. However, Engineer shall not, during such visits or as a result of such observations of Contractor's work in progress, supervise, direct, or have control over the Contractor's Work nor shall Engineer have authority over or responsibility for the means, methods, techniques, sequences, or procedures of construction selected or used by Contractor, for security or safety at the Site, for safety precautions and programs incident to the Contractor's work in progress, for any failure of Contractor to comply with Laws and Regulations applicable to Contractor's performing and furnishing the Work, or responsibility for Contractor's failure to furnish and perform the Work in accordance with the Contract Documents. In addition, the specific terms set forth in section A.1.05 of Exhibit A of the Agreement are applicable.

This clause may not be reproduced without permission of EJCDC.

Exhibit D1.01.D of EJCDC E-500 further provides:

> Resident Project Representative shall not:
>
> . . .
>
> 5. Advise on, issue directions, or assume control over safety practices, precautions, and programs in

> connection with the activities or operations of Owner or Contractor.

<small>This clause may not be reproduced without permission of EJCDC.</small>

Conclusions: In some jurisdictions, a design professional contract stating that the design professional has no responsibility for site safety will provide a legal defense against most suits by non-employees alleging site safety responsibility. But in many jurisdictions, courts have looked beyond the terms of the contract to scrutinize the design professional's actions to determine whether the DP assumed responsibility and exercised authority for site safety that was not expressly given to it by contract. For this reason, it is important that the consultant exercise caution in its communications with the contractor with regard to safety concerns or other matters impacting the means, methods, and procedures of the work. The written and oral communication should clearly maintain that the consultant does not have independent authority to make decisions concerning safety, and that only the contractor and the project owner can make decisions regarding it.

As a practical matter, the consultant's contract should expressly state the limitations upon the consultant's authority concerning jobsite safety responsibility and any authority to stop work. This should include a provision stating that the consultant is not responsible for the safety program and procedures of the general contractor or of the project site. It may be advisable to have the owner include a provision in its contract with the general contractor requiring the contractor to indemnify the consultant for any claim arising out of injuries or death of an employee of the contractor.

As explained in the recent Pennsylvania case, *Herczeg v. Hampton Township and Bankson Engineers*, (quoting from another Pennsylvania case), "the great weight of authority supports the rule that an [engineer] does not, by reason of his supervisory authority over construction, assume responsibility for the day-to-day methods utilized by the contractor to complete the construction. The [engineer's] basic duty is to see that his employer gets a finished product which is structurally sound and which conforms to the specifications and standards. Any duty that the [engineer] may have involving safety procedures of the contract must have been specifically assumed by the contract or must have arisen by actions outside the contract. In determining whether the [engineer's] contractual duty to supervise the construction includes the safety practices on the jobsite, the [engineer] may intentionally, or impliedly by his actions, bring the responsibility for safety within his duty of supervision. The factors which would appear to be relevant in any case where an attempt is made to expand the [engineer's] liability beyond the specific provisions of the employment contract are set forth [as follows]:

(1) actual supervision and control of the work;
(2) retention of the right to supervise and control;
(3) constant participation in ongoing activities at the construction site;
(4) supervision and coordination of subcontractors;
(5) assumption of responsibility for safety practices;
(6) authority to issue change orders; and
(7) the right to stop the work."

This list of factors provides a tool with which a design professional may evaluate whether he is assuming responsibilities for site safety either by contract language or by actions in the field.

Standard of Care

Issue: The standard of care required of a design professional is the care and skill ordinarily used by members of his profession practicing under similar circumstances at the same time and in the same locality. Unless the contract between the design professional and client states otherwise, the design professional is not held to a standard of perfection by the courts. Only if you breach this normal standard of care are you deemed to be "negligent."

Discussion: On almost any construction project, there will be some errors and omissions in plans and specifications. Some of these errors and omissions may cause the owner or the contractor to incur additional costs in completing the job. That does not necessarily mean the owner can recover these extra costs from the design professional. Not every mistake, error, or omission is a negligent one. It is possible, consequently, that the owner may incur additional costs due to your error (e.g., change order costs paid to the contractor), and not be entitled to recover those costs from you. Unless the mistake resulted from your "negligence," you will not be legally responsible to your client for the increased costs it paid to the contractor.

Expert witness testimony is typically required before a design professional can be found negligent. The expert must testify as to the applicable standard of care, and to how you breached that standard and caused the client to suffer damages. The client may not prevail against you unless the jury (or judge, in the event there is no jury) decides, based on the expert testimony, that you were negligent.

Where a contract contains an article holding the design professional to the "highest professional standards for the profession of architects and attaining compliance with applicable local, state and federal law. . . ," this may constitute a warranty or guarantee. It also may create contractual liability for damages that do not arise out of the negligent performance of the insured design professional. Such damages are expressly excluded pursuant to the exclusion section of the insurance policy.

An example from one contract reads as follows:

> *Architect agrees to perform its services in the best and most sound way and in an expeditious and economical manner consistent with the best interests of the Owner.... Upon completion of the Project in accordance with the drawings and specifications, Architect represents that the Project will be a fully functional and integrated facility within the parameters of the Owner's budget for Owner's intended use.*

This language demands services be performed in the "best" way rather than the generally accepted way. Yet, it simultaneously demands that these services be performed expeditiously and in an "economical manner."

Realistically, it may be impossible to be fast, economical, and the "best." Moreover, the owner has included language requiring a "fully functional, integrated facility" meeting the Owner's "intended use." This language could be interpreted to require a uniform commercial code (UCC) type warranty of fitness for intended purpose. In multiple ways, the clause has created uninsurable risk for the design professional.

An additional problem with the "highest standard of care" is that it is confusing and ambiguous. No one can know what the highest standard of care is. The insured design professional has agreed to perform beyond the generally accepted standard of care. This means that he will be unable to defend himself with expert testimony to prove he was not negligent.

Such expert testimony, even if successful in proving the design professional was not negligent, would not necessarily prevail against the breach of contract cause of action brought by the client based on the design professional's failure to perform to the highest standard. Thus, the design professional could be found liable and not have the benefit of insurance to cover its liability.

Beware that project owners, in an apparent effort to obtain their project for the initial budget, are increasingly seeking to make the design firm responsible for contractors' change order costs. To do this, the owner may seek to eliminate your defense that you met the standard of care. Here is an example from a contract:

> If errors and omissions in the project are detected in the plans and specifications, the costs of any re-design required to incorporate the item or feature omitted or correct the error shall be borne by the Architect/Engineer. ... It is generally recognized that the standard of care requires the A/E to be accountable for excessive errors and/or omissions. Therefore, Owner and A/E shall keep a record of costs incurred resulting from A/E's errors and omissions. For each Project, if the accumulation cost of A/E's errors and omissions should exceed the percent of the Cost of the Work agreed and stipulated in the Letter of Engagement, Owner may require the A/E to participate financially to help defray all or some of the excess costs.

In the next example, a project owner begins the standard of care clause with language that looks fairly benign. The clause, however, concludes with language that contradicts the normal standard and makes the design firm responsible for each and every redesign or corrective work—even if the designer was not negligent. The clause reads as follows:

> The Architect agrees to exercise the generally accepted standard of care to complete the Project.... While the Architect shall be liable for its negligence and the negligence of its Subconsultants, the Architect shall perform all redesign or corrective work, at the Architect's own expense, to correct any and all errors, omissions, inconsistencies, or ambiguities (negligent or otherwise) in its design or other Services.

Some project owners may change the standard of care without even mentioning the words "standard of care." This may enable them to hide deep inside a contract some language that completely changes the standard. If you aren't paying attention to this fact, you might mistakenly ask your lawyer or insurance agent to review the risk allocation sections of your contract for insurability and completely miss the key clause they need to review. Consider the following clause that was hidden in the article of the contract titled "Miscellaneous":

> The Official reserves the right, should proof of Defective Services be discovered after final payments, to claim and recover from the Architect and the Architect's professional liability insurer, or either of them, sufficient sums to cover any and all damages, losses or expenses, whether direct, indirect or consequential, arising out of, relating to or in any way connected with the Defective Services.

Another clause of the same contract defined "Defective Services" as follows: "Services that, in the sole discretion of the Official (a) are, or when completed will be, in error, unsatisfactory, deficient or lacking...."

The combination of the above two clauses gives the Owner unfettered discretion to say in its sole opinion that something about the designer's services is unsatisfactory. There is no requirement that the services be negligent in order for them to be deemed unsatisfactory. Any arbitrary reason will do. While the Owner may be able to recover these types of costs from the design firm pursuant to this contractual liability provision, the design firm's insurance carrier is not obligated to pay these costs. A design firm that signs this contract may be found to be in breach of contract for promising insurance coverage that its carrier declines to provide.

Conclusion: Explain to your clients that when they change the standard of care, they create uninsurable risks for you and problems for themselves in trying to recover under your policy. Clients generally understand that they are dependent upon the design professional's insurance policy since design professionals don't have substantial assets. Since the language of this clause creates an uninsurable risk, the client has gained nothing by it. The clause may instead cause an unnecessary dispute over coverage.

A more reasonable clause establishing the standard of care is the following:

> The consultant will perform its services using that degree of care and skill ordinarily exercised under similar conditions by professional consultants

> practicing in the same field at the same time in the same or similar locality.

This clause is not intended for use without advice of counsel.

Another sentence can be added to the end of the above-quoted paragraph to further limit the extent of potential liability:

> No other warranty, express or implied, is made or intended related to the services provided. The Consultant shall only be liable for its own negligent acts or omissions and assumes no liability for the acts or omissions of the Client or other parties.

This clause is not intended for use without advice of counsel.

The EJCDC E-500 (2002), Section 6.01 A, establishes the standard of care for the engineer and expressly disclaims any express or implied warranties. It provides as follows:

> The standard of care for all professional engineering and related services performed or furnished by Engineer under this Agreement will be the care and skill ordinarily used by members of the subject profession practicing under similar circumstances at the same time and in the same locality. Engineer makes no warranties, express or implied, under this Agreement or otherwise, in connection with Engineer's services.

This clause may not be reproduced without permission of EJCDC.

The AIA B141-1997 addresses the issue of exercising reasonable care to meet time schedules for the project in Section 1.2.3.2 as follows:

> The Architect's services shall be performed as expeditiously as is consistent with professional skill and care and the orderly progress of the project. The Architect shall submit for the Owner's approval a schedule for the performance of the Architect's services which shall initially be consistent with the time periods established in Subparagraph 1.1.2.6. . . . Time limits established by this schedule approved by the Owner shall not, except for reasonable cause, be exceeded by the Architect or Owner.

This clause may not be reproduced without permission of AIA.

Termination

Issue: There will generally be a clause providing for termination of your services—both for cause and for the convenience of the owner. When these clauses are drafted by project owners, however, they are not always reciprocal. As a result, they may not provide the design professional with equal rights to terminate the contract, with appropriate compensation for the costs and loss caused by the termination, or adequate protection against reuse of any documentation the design firm may have provided the owner prior to the termination.

Discussion: Design professionals sometimes fail to pay adequate attention to the termination provisions of the agreement—perhaps thinking this is not a key area of risk management. They consequently fail to have their risk managers, insurance brokers, and attorneys evaluate whether onerous conditions in these clauses will create unreasonable risks.

If the client wants the right to terminate the design firm for default, the contract needs to specify a notice requirement as well as a reasonable time to respond to the default notice. Default termination provisions should permit each party to terminate the contract for the other party's default. Termination for convenience, on the other hand, may be a right given only to the owner and not to the design professional—depending upon the nature of the agreement.

Where the agreement is a master services agreement under which the design firm has a long-term contract with its client but only performs services as assigned under work orders, it may be appropriate to permit the designer as well as the owner to terminate the master services agreement if services will not be impacted on existing work orders. An example of such a clause is as follows:

> This Agreement may be terminated for convenience by either party upon 30 days' written notice to the other party, provided that if Consulting Firm has not yet fully discharged its obligations under this Agreement with respect to any pending Services initiated via a Work Order under this Agreement, then such termination shall not occur until all of such obligations have been discharged to the satisfaction of Arch. Upon termination, the Consulting Firm shall submit its final invoice for all reasonable and approved professional fees and reimbursable expenses.

One significant issue arising out of terminated services is what happens to an Instruments of Service the design firm may have given the owner prior to termination. In some instances, owners have even demanded as part of the termination process that the design professional provide them with interim drawings and documents. For a discussion of concerns with reuse of documents, see the section of this book entitled, "Ownership and Use of Documents."

Review owner-generated termination clauses carefully to be sure they don't require you to give your client ownership of your documents. It is likewise important to be sure the client is not entitled by the language to get your draft or interim plans and use those plans with another design professional to complete the project. Limitations should be placed upon use of documents and protection of the terminated design professional.

Conclusion: Include language in your contract similar to that of the AIA and EJCDC documents, providing that either party may terminate for cause, and providing for appropriate financial consideration for the design firm in event of termination.

The EJCDC E-200 (2005), Paragraph 6.05.B, provides in part as follows:

> The obligation to provide further services under this Agreement may be terminated:
>
> 1. For cause,
>
>   a. By either party upon 30 days written notice in the event of substantial failure by the other party to perform in accordance with the terms hereof through no fault of the terminating party.
>
>   b. By Engineer:
>
>   1) upon seven days written notice if Owner demands that Engineer furnish or perform services contrary to Engineer's responsibilities as a licensed professional; or
>
>   2) upon seven days written notice if the Engineer's services for the Project are delayed or suspended for more than 90 days for reasons beyond Engineer's control.
>
>   3) Engineer shall have no liability to Owner on account of such termination.

*****

[Provisions for Remedying Default]

******

2. For convenience,

> a. By Owner effective upon Engineer's receipt of notice from Owner.

<small>This clause may not be reproduced without permission of EJCDC.</small>

Section 6.05.E of EJCDC E-500 also provides for payments upon termination as follows:

> In the event of any termination under Paragraph 6.05, Engineer will be entitled to invoice Owner and to receive full payment for all services performed or furnished and all Reimbursable Expenses incurred through the effective date of termination. Upon making such payment, Owner shall have the limited right to the use of Documents, at Owner's sole risk, subject to the provisions of Paragraph 6.03.E.

<small>This clause may not be reproduced without permission of EJCDC.</small>

The final subparagraph (4) of this section states that where the owner terminates the Engineer for convenience, the Engineer is entitled to payment of a reasonable amount for services and expenses directly attributable to termination, "both before and after the effective date of termination, such as reassignment of personnel, costs of terminating contracts with Engineer's Consultants, and other related close-out costs."

Language like that of the EJCDC document is appropriate to protect the design professional against risks that may be otherwise unmanageable and uninsurable.

Time Limitations on Litigation

Issue: Statutes of limitations and repose may limit the amount of time an injured party has to file suit against a design professional. There is much uncertainty, however, under these statutes regarding when a suit can be filed even if many years have passed since design and construction were completed.

Discussion: To better manage and price the risks associated with design services, design professionals often include language in their contracts establishing a specific limitation on how long a client can wait before filing suit against the design professional for damages arising out of the professional services.

In one case, an appellate court in Maryland affirmed the lower court decision to grant summary judgment because even though the Maryland courts apply the "discovery rule," the parties to a contract are free to negotiate a specific time period for filing suit. The court stated its reluctance to strike down voluntary bargains on public policy grounds. In fact, the court stated that this would be done "only in those cases where the challenged agreement is patently offensive to the public good ...."

As further explained by the court, "In light of this established judicial commitment to protecting individuals' efforts to structure their own affairs through contract, we cannot conclude that the Maryland Court of Appeals would decline to allow parties to contract around the state's default rule establishing the date on which a relevant statute of limitations begins to run."

Conclusion: By establishing a definite cut-off time for your client to sue you, you can limit your risk to a specific

248 *Contract Guide for Design Professionals*

period of time. On construction projects where plaintiffs have sought recovery 25 years or more after project completion, this relief is important. This type of time limitation may reduce your insurance costs since you may not need professional liability insurance coverage for as many years after a project is completed. For design professionals maintaining practice policies with retroactive insurance coverage dates going back many years, this may reduce the premium charged by the carrier.

AIA B141-1997, Section 1.3.7.3, provides:

> Causes of action between the parties to this Agreement pertaining to acts or failures to act shall be deemed to have accrued and the applicable statutes of limitations shall commence to run not later than either the date of Substantial Completion for acts or failures to act occurring prior to Substantial Completion or the date of issuance of the final Certificate for Payment for acts or failures to act occurring after Substantial Completion. In no event shall such statutes of limitations commence to run any later than the date when the Architect's services are substantially completed.

This clause may not be reproduced without permission of AIA.

This AIA language would prevent a party from suing an Architect 25 years after a project was completed even if that party did not discover its damages until that late date.

Similar to AIA B141-1997, EJCDC E-500 (2002) provides that the date of Substantial Completion will start the clock running for any statutory time periods. It provides as follows at Section 6.11.E:

> Accrual of Claims. To the fullest extent permitted by law, all causes of action arising under this Agreement shall be deemed to have accrued, and all statutory periods of limitation shall commence, no later than the date of Substantial Completion.

This clause may not be reproduced without permission of EJCDC.

Another approach is to establish in the Agreement a specified period of time for filing suit against the design professional. Such a provision goes beyond setting Substantial Completion as the date for calculating when the time periods begin to run. An example is the following:

> All actions against the Consultant arising out of negligence, breach of contract, breach of warranty or any other cause however denominated, shall be barred two (2) years from the time claimant knew or should have known of its claim, provided, however, that in no event shall any action be brought more than four years following Substantial Completion of Consultant's services.

This clause is not intended for use without advice of counsel.

Beware that some states may have laws prohiting you from contractually shortening the time periods set by statue. Check with legal counsel in the appropriate state to determine what is permitted and how best to state it in your contract so as to be enforceable.

Waiver of Subrogation

Issue: Insurance companies vary in how they treat a waiver of subrogation. The typical policy states something like the following:

> *Subrogation*
>
> *In the event of any payment under this Policy, WE shall be subrogated to all YOUR rights of recovery against any person or organization and YOU shall execute and deliver instruments and papers and do whatever else is necessary to secure such rights. YOU shall do nothing to prejudice such rights.*

Discussion: Some policies, however, add an exception to this prohibition against waving subrogation—stating that if you are required by your contract to waive subrogation, the carrier will agree to that. Such an exception is provided by the following language:

> *WE shall not exercise any such right against any persons, firms or corporations included in the definition of an INSURED or against YOUR clients if prior to the CLAIM, a waiver of subrogation was so required and accepted under a specific contractual undertaking by YOU.*

Conclusion: Review your policy to determine what is required of you with regard to waiver of subrogation. If your carrier does not permit it, you should advise your client that the waiver is not available. In the alternative, if your policy does not automatically include the waiver of subrogation when it is required by your contracts, you may be able to obtain an endorsement to the policy on a client-by-client or project-by-project basis.

Warranties and Guarantees

Issue: By agreeing to warrant that your professional services will produce an error-free design, you may be contractually liable based on breach of warranty even though you were not negligent in your performance. Professional liability insurance is intended to cover only those damages that arise out of your negligent performance. It does not cover express warranties and guarantees.

Discussion: Some clients are including clauses in their form contracts treating design professionals more like construction contractors than design professionals. Consider this language, for example:

> *Architect warrants and represents that it will take total responsibility for errors and omissions on its documentation and will rectify all such instances at no additional cost to Owner.*

The architect, pursuant to the above warranty, agrees to a higher standard of care than the normal negligence standard. The firm is agreeing to perfection. But no one is perfect. There will be some errors and omissions on any project. As explained in other sections of this book, the owner is expected to pay for such matters in the absence of negligence on the part of the Architect. That is standard industry practice.

In an owner-generated contract for engineering services, the engineer was to agree not only to the highest standard of care but also that the services would be "fit for the purposes intended" by the client. The clause provided the following:

Engineer warrants that the Services shall be performed in accordance with the terms of this Contract and all applicable federal, state and local laws, ordinances and governmental rules and regulations; and the highest standards of professional engineers performing similar services; and that the project of the Services shall be fit for the purposes intended by Client. If, during performance of the Services or within one (1) year after completion of the Services or termination of this Contract or the applicable Request for Services, any portion of the Services or its performance fails to conform to the requirements of the sentence above, Engineer shall promptly correct, at Engineer's own expense, such a nonconformance after receipt of a written notice from Client which shall be given within thirty (30) days. With respect to such corrections, the requirements of the first sentence of this article shall continue for an additional one (1) year period.

Another contract contained a clause that would create Uniform Commercial Code (UCC) type warranties of the professional services. Consider this clause:

Design Professional warrants that its Services shall result in a design that will allow for the successful operation of the Facility, including the suitability of the Project for the use for which the Project is intended.

This creates a warranty of fitness for intended purpose, much like a UCC warranty. This is very dangerous.

A significant problem with giving a warranty may be that it has the potential to extend the statute of limitations period by which the owner may sue the design professional.

A tort action based in negligence must typically be filed within two years (varies by state) whereas a breach of contract (e.g., warranty) may typically be filed for up to six years. For this reason, even when the warranty language does not directly impact the extent of the liability, it is still good risk management practice to eliminate such language from contracts.

Conclusion: Carefully read the contract language provided by your client so that you don't inadvertently agree to warranties and guarantees. Remember that there is an exclusion in the policy for express warranties and guarantees. Some clauses have the same impact as a warranty or guarantee even though they don't expressly contain warranty and guarantee language. If, for example, you agree to the "highest standard of care" instead of the "generally accepted standard," you may have agreed to a hidden warranty that your services will be the best and will produce a perfect result.

Even if you prove at trial that you weren't negligent, you might still be liable for breaching your contractual obligation to meet the "highest standard of care." The professional liability policy will not cover you for that type of breach of contract damages. A project owner needs to understand that it does not need to obtain a warranty from you and that, in fact, it may have better results recovering insurance proceeds for damages if it doesn't have a warranty provision.

If a client sues you for breach of warranty without also suing for negligence, there probably is no insurance company duty to defend. Likewise, if your client recovers from you based on breach of warranty and there is no negligence on your party, the insurance will not cover that recovery. The warranty exclusion of the policy excludes coverage for such losses.

Other clauses that may create warranties by their subtle (or not so subtle language) include those pertaining to "Compliance with Law," which requires you in absolute terms to comply with every law and regulation. If your client incurs damages because you incorrectly interpret and apply a law or regulation, you will be liable for those damages even though your interpretation (although incorrect) was a reasonable one. Only if your interpretation was negligent will your professional policy cover the damages. Explain this to your client and seek to add language to the clause stating that you will "exercise reasonable care" to comply with the applicable laws and regulations.

A clause addressing "Cost Estimates" can also create a potential warranty situation. Agree only to exercise reasonable care in preparing the cost estimates. A clause that requires you to certify that the construction contractor completed all the work in conformance with the plans and specifications also creates uninsurable warranties. It might constitute a warranty-type assurance to the client that the contractor has completed the work in a satisfactory manner, and this may create liability for you if it is later determined that the contractor did not perform in complete accordance with all the plans and specifications.

EJCDC Document E-500, Section 6.01 A, provides:

> The standard of care for all professional engineering and related services performed or furnished by Engineer under this Agreement will be the care and skill ordinarily used by members of the subject profession practicing under similar circumstances at the same time and in the same locality. Engineer makes no warranties, express or implied, under this

Warranties and Guarantees

> Agreement or otherwise, in connection with Engineer's services.

This clause may not be reproduced without permission of EJCDC.

When it comes to warranties and guarantees, design firms need to explain to their clients that the warranty exclusion of the professional liability policy will deny them coverage for costs related to such warranties and guarantees. Having warranties in your contract might so confuse the question of liability that it could adversely impact the insurance company's ability to defend a claim and analyze whether any coverage for negligence might be applicable to the matter. With that in mind, a project owner may want to reconsider the wisdom of including warranties and guarantees in its design professional contracts.

Chapter 11

Continuing Education Courses

10.1 Communication, Documentation & Site Safety: Risk Management for Design Professionals
10.2 Site Safety & Contract Issues
10.3 Design Professional Contracts & Insurance

These three courses may be taken through the end of 2007. After that, contact a/e ProNet before submitting answers and payment.

Continuing Education: Course 1

Communication, Documentation & Site Safety: Risk Managagement for Design Professionals

This course has been submitted to the American Institute of Architects (AIA) Continuing Education System (CES) as a two learning unit course. The a/e ProNet, an AIA registered provider of continuing education, will issue you a certificate of course completion if you read the text of this Guide from pages 1-38, 199-204, and 221-232 of the Risk Management & Contract Guide for Design Professionals and submit an answer sheet, along with your **payment in the amount of $49.95** to a/e ProNet at 3543 Somerset Circle, Kissimmee, FL 34746. If you have questions concerning the course, please send e-mail to: info@aeProNet.org. You must sign your answer sheet and include the certification provided at the conclusion of the last question below. Answer each question:

1. Risk managers often speak of three primary means of risk management: risk avoidance, risk allocation, and risk reduction.
a) True; b) False

2. In allocating risks by contract terms and conditions, the goal of the parties should be to allocate the specific risks to the party with the best ability to manage them.
a) True; b) False

3. When sending an important notice or recommendation to a client, which of the following may constitute of a written record of the communication?
a) a fax confirmation notice,
b) an e-mail confirmation notice,
c) a certified mail-return receipt,
d) all of the above.

4. Standard form contracts for both construction and design professional services generally state the terms under which a firm may rely upon site information provided by the client. Contracts, generated by some project owners, however, may include language stating that any site condition information provided by the owner is done so merely for general information and shall not be deemed a part of the contract or relied upon by designers or contractors.
a) True; b) False

5. Contract language denying a contractor's right to rely on site information documentation may cause an increase in project costs, claims and litigation because:
a) Bidders that are contractually barred from relying upon information provided with the IFB may seek to include in their bids extra costs for unknown site condition contingencies.
b) To get around the contract provision, contractors may seek creative ways to make themselves whole – such as asserting fault on the part of the design professional.
c) Both of the above answers may be correct.

6. If you are entitled to rely upon documentation and site data provided to you by the client when you are preparing your proposal, which of the following is true:
a) By maintaining proposal or bid worksheets showing how you prepared your proposal in reliance upon data from the owner, may help you demonstrate detrimental reliance upon that data in the event of a subsequent claim.

b) By referring to owner-provided data in your proposal, you may be able to demonstrate the underlying assumptions upon which you have based your proposal and if the owner subsequently demands that you perform services differing from what was anticipated, you may be able to use the data (and the fact that you referred to it and relied upon it) to prove that you are being required to perform additional services entitling you to additional fee.
c) Both of the statements in (a) and (b) may be correct.

7. Which of the following is suggested in the Guide concerning recommendations made by the design professional to the project owner:
a) Put recommendations in writing, including an explanation of the potential benefits of following the recommendations and the potential risks of failing to do so.
b) If alternative solutions or recommendations are available, conveying that information to the client, in writing, facilitates informed and well-reasoned decisions by the client.
c) Enough detail should be provided in the written recommendation so that the client cannot assert that it did not understand the ramifications of the decision it was making.
d) All of the above.

8. In one of the two HVAC cases referenced in the Guide, the architect said the owner overruled its advice to reject "or equal" equipment. The owner argued that although the architect advised it to reject the equipment, the recommendation was not adequate because the architect's language did not contain facts, figures, or data to persuade it to reject the equipment.
a) True; (b) False

9. If the client does not respond in writing to your recommendation, it may be advisable to follow-up with a memorandum such as a "speed memo," fax, or e-mail to the client reiterating that you gave him a written recommendation, and mentioning any conversations you and the client may have had pertaining to that recommendation and any related decisions that were made by the client.
a) True; b) False

10. Which of the following would be the *least* effective way to reduce the risks associated with issuing a report containing your professional opinions concerning a property condition assessment?
a) state the foundation and assumptions, including information provided by the client that underly your opinions.
b) state the impact of any time limitations imposed upon your review
c) identify limitations on information that could be obtained
d) certify that your opinion is accurate and provide a guarantee if requested.

11. Which records are ordinarily given the most evidentiary weight by courts?
a) Records that are created and maintained contemporaneously in the ordinary course of business
b) Records created by attorneys for the parties during arbitration or litigation after the project has been built..

12. If you use your home computer to do work on a project for your employer, which of the following statements is true?
a) If your employer is subject to a discovery request during litigation concerning the project, the employer is required to provide the requester with access to the project records located on your computer.
b) As long as you don't bring your computer to work, you and your employer will not have to provide content from it during a discovery request during litigation.
c) If your employer is subject to a discovery request concerning the project, you should promptly erase all relevant documentation from your computer.

13. If your office has a formal document retention policy, you may delete e-mail from your system and erase it from any back-up tapes or other disks, computers, and servers in a manner consistent with your corporate records purging/retention policy, even though the records are pertinent to a claim or litigation that has been filed and even though a document discovery request has been filed seeking those same documents.
a) True; b) False

14. Which of the following suggestions concerning e-mail is not made in the Guide?
a) Be careful what you write. Think before you automatically type the first thoughts that go through your mind.
b) Don't be too informal.
c) Check your spelling and grammar—including punctuation—before you click "send."
d) Print each e-mail, regardless of significance, and save it in a file

15. Which of the following suggestions concerning e-mail is made in the Guide?
a) E-mail correspondence and requests to the project owner can always be used in place of contracutally defined procedures for requesting information and approvals of changes.
b) It is permissible to add additional services to your scope based on e-mails from people who do not have the contractual authority to assign additional services or approve change orders.
c) Organize important, significant, e-mail into electronic folders for easy access and retrieval.
d) All of the above.

16. As a general rule, the Guide suggests that if a statute of repose applies to your services or work, you should maintain significant project records at least through the end of the time period established under that statute.
a) True; b) False

17. When you receive a document production request in the course of a claim or litigation, you are expected to provide copies or access to documents relevant to the request whether they are in an "official file," or "working files," desk drawers, job-site trailers, workers' homes, or computers at the office and home.
a) True; b) False

18. Some of the factors considered by the courts in deciding whether to impose liability for negligently destroying evidence include the following:
a) there was a duty to maintain the evidence imposed either by law or contract;
b) a potential claim or law suit existed;

c) the ability of the plaintiff to prove its case has been significantly impaired by the destruction of documentation;
d) all of the above.

19. A records retention policy designed and carried out in good faith in the ordinary course of business, prior to the initiation of litigation may provide a defense to claims of spoliation of evidence.
a) True; b) False

20. Construction contracts such as standard AIA contract forms expressly state that the contractor has responsibility for site safety. The design professional contract form typically states that the design professional is not responsible for site safety, and that the construction contractor has sole responsibility for it.
a) True; b) False

21. Where the design professional has involved itself in site safety decisions and exercised control over the work or workers' safety, some courts have held the design professional to be responsible for site safety based on its actions in the field that created implied authority to control the work despite the contract language to the contrary.
a) True; b) False

22. In the case of Carvalho v. Toll Brothers and Developers, the court held that when an engineer has actual knowledge of a laborer working in an imminently dangerous condition, the engineer has a duty to take some action to avoid laborer injury.
a) True; b) False

23. In the case of Herczeg v. Hampton Township Municipal Authority and Bankson Engineers, the Pennsylvania court did which of the following:
a) found the engineer liable for site safety;
b) decided to follow the holding of Carvallo as case precedent
c) declined to follow the holding of Carvallo.
d) none of the above.

Continuing Education Courses 265

24. Factors that some courts consider to be relevant in deciding whether the design professional has site safety responsibility beyond the specific provisions of its contract include the following:
a) actual supervision and control of the work;
b) constant participation in ongoing activities at the construction site;
c) assumption of responsibility for safety practices;
d) all of the above.

I hereby certify that I read the content of pages 1-38, 199-204, and 221-232 of the Risk Management & Contract Guide for Design Professionals, and that I have personally read and answered each of the questions contained in the exam for Course 1: Communication, Documentation & Site Safety: Risk Management for Design Professionals.

Signature:_____ Date: _____
Individual Name: _____
Firm Name: _____
Physical Address:_____
Phone:_____
E-mail address:_____
AIA Member Number (if applicable):_____

Continuing Education Course 2:

Design Professional Contract Terms and Conditions, Part I: Risk Allocation & Management

This course has been submitted to the American Institute of Architects (AIA) Continuing Education System (CES) as a **four (4)** learning unit course. The a/e ProNet, an AIA registered provider of continuing education, will issue you a certificate of course completion if you read the text of this Guide from pages 39-66, 73-152, 177-232, and 241-252, and submit an answer sheet, along with your **payment in the amount of $99.95** to a/e ProNet at 3543 Somerset Circle, Kissimmee, FL 34746. If you have questions concerning the course, please send e-mail to: info@aeProNet.org. You must sign your answer sheet and include the certification provided at the conclusion of the last question below.

Answer each multiple choice question:

1. Ava Abramowitz states which of the following:
a) At its most basic, a contract makes the progress of the project predictable.
b) a contract helps the parties achieve their strategic objectives.
c) A contract affords both parties the opportunity to set realistic expectations of the other.
d) none of the above.

2. Contracts can provide the framework that can facilitate future negotiations and contracts can help clarify and solidify the working relationships between the parties.
a) True; b) False

3. Contracts are a private law – a law written by two parties that our public courts will generally enforce.
a) True; b) False

4. Which of the following is true:
a) Parties may enter into legally binding contracts that are oral and never reduced to writing, but it is wise to put professional services agreements in writing to the greatest extent possible.
b) Getting the scope services and fee established in writing can be some of the most critical elements of the contract—to avoid some of the greatest ambiguities and misunderstandings that typically result in disagreement and litigation.
c) Both of the above.

5. If a design firm agrees to assume liability for schedule delays, it may have an uninsured loss if delay results from reasons other than its own negligent acts, errors and omissions..
a) True; b) False

6. When design professionals get too far ahead of their client with services that have not been paid for, and then later try to catch up with their billing and payment, the following may happen?
a) the client may make excuses for why the design professional is not entitled to the full amount due.
b) If the design firm sues its client to collect the balance of fees it believes is due, the client may defend itself by arguing the design professional is not entitled to the fee because it performed its services negligently.
c) If the design firm sues its client to collect the balance of fees it believes is due, the client might counter-sue to recover from the design professional damages for change order costs it paid to the contractor and any other costs the owner asserts were caused by negligent performance.
d) all of the above.

7. Instead of using the standard forms of the AIA or other organizations (that require a royalty for each use of the form), some parties choose to create and use their own contract forms. If you do this, the Guide recommends you have your contract reviewed by the following:
a) an attorney experienced with construction law in your jurisdiction and the locations where your project services will be performed.

b) insurance professionals such as brokers and insurance company personnel.
c) Both (a) and (b).

8. Which of the following may create the *least* risk for the design professional?
a) "supervise contractor's work"
b) "control contractor's work"
c) "direct contractor's work"
c) "Review the contractor's work"

9. Statements and representations contained in promotional materials, such a brochures and web-sites, may potentially create uninsurable warranties, guarantees, or promises of highest standard of services.
a) True; b) False

10. The best way to manage risk is to:
a) avoid it.
b) allocate it to someone else.
c) reduce it through proactive steps of loss control and risk management.
d) any one of the above three may be the most appropriate —it depends upon the circumstances.

11. The party to whom risk should be contractually assigned is the party that:
a) has the most money.
b) has the least bargaining power.
c) is gracious enough to accept the risk.
d) is in the best position to control the risk.

12. Which party is generally the one most logical to assume the responsibility for obtaining easements and rights of ways and the risk of pre-existing site conditions?
a) design professional
b) Owner
c) Contractor
d) Supplier

13. Which party generally should be contractually responsible for the following: (1) Means, methods and procedures of construction to satisfy the contract document requirements (2) Warranties and guarantees of contractor work, and (3) Timeliness of construction performance.
a) design professional
b) Owner
c) Contractor
d) all of the above

14. If you sign a contract committing to comply with all law, or to comply with the Americans with Disabilities Act, which of the clauses below would most appropriately state your commitment in a manner that can satisfy the client's need but not create uninsurable risk for you?
a) You "will comply with all requirements...."
b) You will "do your best to comply with all requirements...."
c) You will "exercise the generally accepted standard of care to comply with applicable requirements...."
d) none of the above.

15. To protect against someone relying upon electronic drawings that have been altered or have become corrupted, which of the following would afford the greatest protection?
a) Use a reliable CAD program.
b) Use a reliable web-based project management system.
c) Mandate by contract language that the controlling instrument of service will be hard copy drawings.

16. Protections for the design professional with regard to the use of electronic data include which of the following:
a) Contract language stating the hard copy documents will be the benchmark and controls over any conflicting CADD or electronic document.
b) Contract language limiting the purposes for which the information may be used and who may use it.
c) Contractual indemnification by any person who uses the electronic information for purposes other than those expressly agreed upon in the contract.
d) All of the above.

17. The design professional liability policy will potentially cover construction costs that exceed the project budget if:
a) The design professional contractually agreed to take responsibility for the cost overruns but did not negligently cause the the cost overrun.
b) The design professional warranted the estimate but did not negligently cause the overrun.
c) The overruns were directly caused by negligence of the design professional in performing professional services.

18. Which of the following statements is most accurate:
a) Mediation is generally a form conflict resolution to produce a voluntary settlement.
b) Mediation generally produces decisions by a mediation panel that are binding on the parties.
c) Arbitration is always preferable to litigation.
d) If mediation fails to resolve a dispute, the parties are typically precluded from taking the matter to further resolution methods such as arbitration or litigation.

19. The lack of a decision by arbitrators explaining the factual and legal basis for their decision may make it difficult or impossible to determine whether an award against the design professional arises out of insurable causes such as negligent errors.
a) True
b) False

20. Which of the following two certifications creates less potential risk for the consultant?
a) The Consultant will provide a written report stating whether in its opinion, based upon site visits, the construction work complies generally with the design concept.
b) Upon completion of the construction, the Consultant shall certify that the work was completed in accordance with the plans, specifications and drawings.

21. Which of the following is a benefit of including a differing site conditions clause in the contract between the owner and contractor whereby the contractor will be given a change order to recover its

costs of encountering a changed condition or differing site condition?
a) it may reduce the adversarial relationships on the project.
b) it may help change order requests and claims be resolved more expeditiously.
c) by agreeing to compensate the contractor for the additional costs only when the condition is encountered, the owner may actually save money by obtaining more competitive bids that don't contain contingencies to cover costs of differing site conditions that only might be encountered
d) all of the above.

22. It is inappropriate to ever place any limitation upon a design professional's ability to disclose confidential information.
a) True
b) False

23. Of the terms below, which is generally deemed to create the greatest risk for the design professional?
a) observe the contractor's work.
b) monitor the contractor's work.
c) review the contractor's work.
d) inspect the contractor's work.

24. Under the AIA and EJCDC documents for owner-design professional agreements, who owns the copyright to the Instruments of Service?
a) The project owner.
b) The construction contractor.
c) The design professional.
d) The attorneys.

25. Before performing services that you consider to be "additional," which of the following should you do?
a) invoice the client before performing services.
b) obtain written authorization from the designated representative of the client to perform the services.
c) do not agree to perform additional services.
d) obtain either oral or written authorization from someone that is employed by the client.

26. If the scope of the services in your contract does not include responding to environmental conditions, you should:
a) Negotiate language into the Agreement that will protect you in the event that environmental conditions are encountered.
b) Before agreeing to do any environmental related service per a change request, review your insurance policy to determine whether it excludes coverage for pollution liability.
c) In the event that you later respond to a request by the owner to perform services related to pollution found at the project, do not accept responsibility for choosing an off-site disposal facility to dispose of the waste.
d) all of the above.

27. If the contract contains an incorporation by reference clause, the Guide suggests:
a) Don't agree to incorporate by reference the terms of another contract unless you have read that contract and understand those terms.
b) If terms of the incorporated contract conflict with the risk allocation provisions of your subcontract, amend the incorporation clause by adding an exception to incorporation for specific, identified articles of your subcontract.
c) both (a) and (b)
d) neither (a) nor (b).

28. When a contract states that the design professional must give requests for approval of additional services to specific, named individuals, courts never will enforce the requirements so long as the project owner knew about the additional services and was not harmed due to the failure of the design professional to comply with the notice procedures.
a) True
b) False

29. Owners duty to provide data and the design professionals right to rely upon data provided by the project owner is the subject of the following clauses:
a) AIA B141—1997, Article 1.2.3.7
b) EJCDC Document E-500, 6.01.D "Standards of Performance"

274 *Contract Guide for Design Professionals*

c) both (a) and (b)
d) neither (a) nor (b)

30. With regard to ownership and copyright of the design professional's Instruments of Service, the Guide suggests the design professional do the following:
a) maintain the copyright of their documents and give the owner only a limited license to use them for their specific project
b) get contract language stating that the documents are the property of design professionals and are not to be reused without authorization;
c) if permitting the owner to reuse the documents on other projects then obtain indemnification or protection against the risk of liability that might arise out of reuse of the documents.
d) all of the above.

I hereby certify that I read the content of pages 39-66, 73-152, 177-232, and 241-252 of the Risk Management & Contract Guide for Design Professionals, and that I have personally read and answered each of the questions contained in the exam for Course 2: Design Professional Contract Terms and Conditions, Part I: Risk Allocation & Management.

Signature:_____ Date: _____
Individual Name: _____
Firm Name: _____
Physical Address:_____
Phone:_____
E-mail address:_____
AIA Member Number (if applicable):_____

Continuing Education Course 3:

Design Professional Contract Terms and Conditions, Part II: Insurance Issues & Insurability of Indemnification, Scope of Service, Standard of Care, and Warranties

This course has been submitted to the American Institute of Architects (AIA) Continuing Education System (CES) as a **two(2)** learning unit course. The a/e ProNet, an AIA registered provider of continuing education, will issue you a certificate of course completion if you read the text of this Guide from pages 67-71, 153-179, 233-240, and 253-257, and submit an answer sheet, along with your **payment in the amount of $49.95** to a/e ProNet at 3543 Somerset Circle, Kissimmee, FL 34746. If you have questions concerning the course, please send e-mail to: info@aeProNet.org. Your must sign your answer sheet and include the certification provided at the conclusion of the last question below.

1. A design professional's errors and omissions (e & o) policy is intended to cover damages arising out of the insured design professional's:
a) breach of contract.
b) breach of warranty or guarantee.
c) negligence.
d) all mistakes.

2. Damage arising out of which of the following is generally considered uninsurable:
a) intentional wrongdoing.
b) breach of warranty.
c) indemnification for anything other than the design professional's negligence.
d) all of the above.

3. A project owner can generally be named as an "additional insured" on a design professional's errors and omissions policy.
a) True; b) False

4. The typical e & o policy for a design professional is issued on a "claims made" basis.
a) True; b) False

5. If you sign a contract committing to comply with all laws and codes, including the Americans with Disabilities Act, which of the clauses below would most appropriately state your commitment in a manner that can satisfy the client's need but not create uninsurable risk for you?
a) You "will comply with all requirements...."
b) You will "do your best to comply with all requirements...."
c) You will "exercise the generally accepted standard of care to comply with applicable requirements...."
d) none of the above.

6. Construction costs that exceed the project budget would potentially be covered as damages under a professional liability policy only if:
a) the design professional contractually agreed to take responsibility for the cost overruns.
b) the design professional warranted the estimate.
c) the overruns were directly caused by negligence of the design professional in performing professional services.

7. Hypothetically, you have signed a contract agreeing to indemnify your client for "all damages caused in whole or in part from your negligence." The client incurs damages caused 20% by you, 30% by another consultant, 40% by the construction contractor, and 10% by the client. How much of those damages are you potentially responsible for (in many but not necessarily all jurisdictions) under the terms of your indemnification agreement?
a) 20%
b) 50%
c) 90%
d) 100%

8. From the examples of indemnification language below, choose the phrase that a design professional (DP) should deem most acceptable and insurable.

a) "DP will indemnify client for damages arising out of the performance of the services."
b) "DP will indemnify the client for damages arising out of the acts, errors, and omissions of the DP."
c) "DP will indemnify the client for damages arising out of the DP's services unless caused by the sole negligence of the Client."
d) "DP will indemnify the client for damages to the extent caused by the negligent performance of the services by the DP."

9. If you are liable to your client for damages pursuant to the terms of an indemnification clause, what part of those damages may be covered by your professional liability policy?
a) Damages awarded to the client through litigation or arbitration.
b) Damages to the extent caused by any of your acts, errors, and omissions.
c) Damages to the extent caused by your negligent acts, errors, and omissions.
d) Damages caused by breach of warranty and guarantee.

10. One exclusion in the professional liability policy that may prevent coverage for damages arising out of indemnification requirements is commonly know as:
a) The design-build exclusion.
b) The contractual liability exclusion.
c) The defective workmanship exclusion.
d) The site safety exclusion.

11. If the limitation of liability clause is to limit the liability to an amount of insurance, which language will be better for the design professional?
a) "liability is limited to the amount of the insurance proceeds available."
b) "liability is limited to the amount of the insurance proceeds paid by the DP's insurance carrier"
c) "liability is limited to the amount of the insurance required by the contract and available under the policy"

12. In order to more likely withstand judicial scrutiny, a limitation of liability clause should be prominently presented in the contract and should provide a limit that is reasonable in view of the risks.
a) True; b) False

13. What standard of care is applied to the design professional if nothing is stated in the contract about this?
a) The highest standard.
b) No standard.
c) The generally accepted standard of care at the time and place where the services are performed.
d) Perfection.

14. Liability for negligence should not be imposed by a judge or jury unless the design professional is found to have:
a) Breached a warranty.
b) Breached a guarantee.
c) Failed to meet the generally accepted standard of care.
d) Failed to meet the highest standard of care.

15. If the design professional agrees, by contract, to an express warranty, and breaches the warranty as a result of negligent performance of services, which of the following is true under the typical professional liability policy?
a) There will be no coverage under the E&O policy for any of the damages because the "express warranty" exclusion applies.
b) There will be no coverage under the E&O policy for any of the damages because the "contractual liability exclusion" applies.
c) There may be coverage under the E&O policy, but only to the extent of damages caused by negligence of the design professional.
d) All the costs incurred by the design professional will be covered.

16. Agreeing to produce "an error-free design" may constitute a warranty, and if you are found liable for breach of warranty that does not arise from your negligence, you may be liable to your client for damages not covered by your e&o insurance.
a) True; b) False

17. In determining whether you have coverage for specific types of damages under your professional liability policy, you should look at the following section or sections of the policy:
a) Definitions "Damages"
b) Exclusions
c) Endorsements
d) All of the above

18. With regard to waiver of subrogation, professional liability insurance policies consistently prohibit the insured design professionals from waiving subrogation in favor of their clients.
a) True; b) False

I hereby certify that I read the content of pages 67-71, 153-179, 233-240, and 253-257 of the Risk Management & Contract Guide for Design Professionals, and that I have personally read and answered each of the questions contained in the exam for Course 3: Design Professional Contract Terms and Conditions, Part II: Insurance Issues & Insurability of Indemnification, Scope of Service, Standard of Care, and Warranties.

Signature:_____ Date: _____
Individual Name: _____
Firm Name: _____
Physical Address:_____
Phone:_____
E-mail address:_____
AIA Member Number (if applicable):_____

Index

Additional insureds 70, 170
Additional Services 48, 211
AIA contract documents 52, 53-58
Alternative Dispute Resolution 131
Americans With Disabilities Act (ADA) 77, 111
Arbitration 137
Abramowitz, Ava 39
Basic Services 47, 211
CAD and Electronic Media 81
Certifications 87
Changes in Design Professional's Services 91
Change Orders for Construction Work 97
Changed Conditions (Differing Site Conditions) 103
Choice of Law & Venue 107
Claims reporting requirements 131
Compliance with Law 111
Communication between parties 11
Confidentiality 117
Consequential damages 174
Continuing education courses 259
Contract
        AIA documents 52, 53-58
        Basic elements 47
        Client-developed 62
        DBIA documents 58
        Do's and Don'ts 63
        EJCDC documents 52
        Essentials 45
        Example clauses 77
        Fee schedule 49
        General terms and conditions 51
        Get it in writing 45
        Key Concepts 42
        Negotiations 24

Owner-generated form 62
Purpose 39
Schedule 48
Scope of service 47
Standard forms 51
Words to avoid 64
Contract essentials 45
Contractual liability exclusion 67-68, 171
Copyright ownership 187
Cost Estimates 123
DBIA contract documents 58
Damages 127
Defending the client 153
Delays 205
Differing site conditions 103
Discovery in litigation 32
Dispute Resolution 131
Documentation issues 5
Drawings 187
EJCDC contract documents 52
Electronic media 81
E-mail 26-29, 35
Environmental Conditions 143
Errors and omissions 169
Estimate of project costs 121
Excluded services 212
Fee schedule 49
Harness, Suzanne 53
Holland, Kent ii
Hazardous materials 144
Hold harmless provisions 153
Incorporation by Reference 149
Indemnification 68, 153-161
Information provided by others 199
Inspection 163
Insurance 67, 169-172
 Contractual Liability exclusion 67

    Indemnification provision affected 68
    Who is covered 70
Instruments of Service 187
Jobsite safety 221
Joinder of parties 141
Limitation of Liability 173
Loulakis, Michael C. 58
Marketing and promotional materials 65
Mediation 134
Negligence 233
Notice Requirements 177
Observation of work 163-167, 226
Owner Provided Data 181
Ownership and Copyrights of Documents 187
Performance schedule 48
Permits and approvals 195
Pre-bid data 8
Professional opinions - foundation 14
Professional liability insurance 67
Proof of communication 12
Records attorney-client privilege 23
Records destruction 33
Records discovery 32
Records maintenance 21, 33-37
Records organization 22
Records retention 19, 31
Records web-based 25
Requests for Information 209
Rejection of work 230
Reuse of documents 187
Reliance on Information Provided by Others 199
Responsibility for the Services of Others 203
Right to stop work 231
Risk allocation 3
Risk avoidance 1
Risk management 1
Risk reduction 4

Safety 221
Schedule (Timeliness of Performance) 205
Schedule - contractor's responsibility 207
Scope of Service 211
Severability & Survival 213
Shop Drawings 217
Site Safety 221
Spoliation of evidence 33
Standard form contracts 51
Standard of Care 233
Termination 241
Time Limitations on Litigation 247
Time of the essence 205
Timeliness of performance 205
Uniform Commercial Code 234
Waiver of consequential damages 174
Waiver of Subrogation 251
Warranties and Guarantees 69, 253-257
Web-based documentation 25